The Definitive Guide to Getting a Teaching Job

An Insider's Guide to Finding the Right Job, Writing the Perfect Resume, and Nailing the Interview

Mary C. Clement

ROWMAN & LITTLEFIELD EDUCATION
Lanham, Maryland • Toronto • Plymouth, UK
2007

ROWMAN & LITTLEFIELD EDUCATION

Published in the United States of America
by Rowman & Littlefield Education
A Division of Rowman & Littlefield Publishers, Inc.
A wholly owned subsidiary of The Rowman & Littlefield Publishing Group, Inc.
4501 Forbes Boulevard, Suite 200, Lanham, Maryland 20706
www.rowmaneducation.com

Estover Road
Plymouth PL6 7PY
United Kingdom

British Library Cataloguing in Publication Information Available

Library of Congress Cataloging-in-Publication Data

Clement, Mary C.
  The definitive guide to getting a teaching job : an insider's guide to finding the right
job, writing the perfect resume, and nailing the interview / Mary C. Clement.
    p. cm.
  Includes bibliographical references.
  ISBN-13: 978-1-57886-605-2 (hardcover : alk. paper)
  ISBN-10: 1-57886-605-7 (hardcover : alk. paper)
  ISBN-13: 978-1-57886-606-9 (pbk. : alk. paper)
  ISBN-10: 1-57886-606-5 (pbk. : alk. paper)
  1. Teachers—Employment—United States—Handbooks, manuals, etc. 2. Teaching—
Vocational guidance—United States—Handbooks, manuals, etc. 3. Job hunting—United
States—Handbooks, manuals, etc. I. Title.
  LB1780.C474 2007
  371.10023'73—dc22

2007005426

∞™ The paper used in this publication meets the minimum requirements of
American National Standard for Information Sciences—Permanence of
Paper for Printed Library Materials, ANSI/NISO Z39.48-1992.
Manufactured in the United States of America

This book is lovingly dedicated to my aunt, Miss Mary M. Butler, who taught me the value of finding a job and working hard at it.

Contents

1

Becoming a Teacher

TEACHERS AND THEIR JOBS

If you have picked up this book, you have probably been a student for 13 to 17 years. As a student, you have seen 40 to 70 teachers do their jobs. You are a valid evaluator of those teachers because you know which ones were good and which ones should never have been hired. So, now you are planning to join the noble profession of teaching! Let's talk about what teachers really do and the reasons people become teachers.

THIS BOOK IS WRITTEN FOR YOU IF . . .

This book is written for you if you are a college student in an education program and need to know the nuts and bolts of how to find your first job. If you have a college degree but it doesn't include a teaching license, then this book will help you understand the maze of teacher certification and how (and if) you can get a teaching job with only your current degree. There are teaching jobs available for people without college degrees, especially in the areas of preschool education and substitute teaching, and this book will help you find those jobs.

Have you been in a career that you are tired of? Want to make a difference in the world, instead of just making money for your mortgage payment? This book will help you change careers and join the teaching profession.

Does your current career involve so much travel and so many late hours that your children don't recognize you? Teaching is considered the most family-friendly profession, and becoming a teacher may give you the much-needed time and flexibility needed to be a parent. Of course, you've got to secure a job before enjoying those benefits.

Are you already a practicing teacher? Do you honestly think that you will stay in your classroom and your current school for the next 30 years? This book will teach you what is new in job searching and interviewing so that you can win a position for a different grade level or subject in your district or get a job in another district.

For all readers—seniors in college or job-changers—this book has the most current information about online job searching and the newest style of teacher interviewing (behavior-based interviewing), and answers to all of your questions about getting from where you are now to being employed as a teacher. The sample cover letters and résumés in chapter 3 will enable you to create paperwork that gets the attention of the employer. The interview questions (and answers) in chapter 5 will help you sell your background and experience to the potential employer.

WHAT TEACHERS REALLY DO

First and foremost, teaching is not for the faint of heart! Teaching is a demanding and challenging job. Imagine for a moment that twenty-two 7-year-olds will be with you in your classroom from 8:15 a.m. until 3:30 p.m. and that you must keep them busy and out of trouble and teach them reading, writing, spelling, math, science, social studies, health, and citizenship. Did I mention that you must also check their heads for lice and watch them for behaviors that might indicate abuse or neglect?

Is teaching older students "easier?" Well, that depends on your definition of easy. A high school teacher will teach five or six 50-minute classes or three 90- to 100-minute classes a day to 14- to 18-year-olds. Secondary teachers give classes in their subject-matter field, like English, math, science, social studies, foreign languages, health, music, or physical education. However, within the field, each teacher may have many different classes to teach—biology, chemistry, and earth science might all be taught by one teacher in a small school, and he or she might teach two classes of each every day. Three classes a day may have advantages—fewer students to teach, to get to know, and fewer papers to grade—but keeping 16-year-olds on task for 90 to 100 minutes a day can be daunting for master teachers.

What about middle grades? (Yes, it used to be called junior high.) A typical day for a middle grades teacher includes teaching the same type of load as a high school teacher but may involve more counseling, homeroom, and student support duties. Since 6th, 7th, and 8th graders may be lacking in basic skills, many middle grades teachers teach reading one hour a day.

Is the teacher's day over when the students leave? No. After school is when the extracurricular duties kick in. Called cocurriculars in some districts, these involve coaching sports, sponsoring academic teams, rehearsing students for plays, and preparing students for college entrance exams at the high school level. Middle school teachers serve as coaches, club sponsors, and counselors after school hours. Elementary teachers are often needed to provide after-school programs, enrichment classes, and sports or gymnastics coaching, too.

Are the teacher's duties done after the after-school duties are finished? The answer is again no. Teachers often take papers home to grade, and there is rarely enough time at school to do all the planning and reading ahead for future lessons. The good news is that a teacher can grade papers and make a pot of chili and do laundry at the same time once he or she gets home. Hence the family-friendliness of teaching!

WHO BECOMES A TEACHER AND WHY

After reading that teachers have challenging days and endless nights of after-school duties, you may be asking, "Who becomes a teacher and why?" Even though many teachers admit the difficulties of teaching, they also admit the joys. Watching a child learn to read and knowing that you made their learning possible is indeed a thrill. Helping a talented teenager graduate and start a job or begin college is also a major delight. It is fun to read stories to 8-year-olds, then watch them act out the story with a new ending. It is truly rewarding to help an at-risk 7th grader raise his achievement in school, knowing that his success will enable him to reach greater successes in high school. Yes indeed, teaching is the toughest job you'll ever love. And if you need another saying to put on your refrigerator to motivate you to teach, here it is: Don't just make a living—make a difference.

PRESCHOOL TEACHERS

There is a huge need for preschool teachers, those who teach 3- to 5-year-olds. Why the need? With more two-income families, both parents need to return to the workforce full-time as soon as possible, making preschools a much more viable option than just day care or babysitting services. Many public schools now offer preschools for children 3 years and older, making preschool a free option. With the growing number of children and the growing number of public preschool programs, the demand is up for teachers. There is actually a shortage of preschool teachers who are trained to teach special needs and special education students.

Preschool teachers choose this age level to teach because of their desire to work with "little ones." Also, some preschool teachers are parents themselves, and sometimes they can arrange shortened workdays or free tuition at a private preschool for their own children as part of their work package. While preschool teachers have tremendous accountability for the physical care of the children, they often do not have the academic accountability associated with teaching at the higher grades. (Examples: Elementary teachers have been sued by parents who think that their child didn't learn to read "on time." Some state policymakers think that teachers' pay should be linked to the standardized test scores. Those are stressful accountability factors for teachers!)

Preschool teachers in private schools are not necessarily certified teachers and therefore do not need a bachelor's degree. Many preschools employ teachers who have earned an associate's degree at a community college in early childhood or child development. The downside is that preschool teachers who do not have a bachelor's degree and certification may only make a fraction of what fully certified teachers will earn.

ELEMENTARY TEACHERS

Most elementary teachers report that they became teachers because they love children. These teachers are often the children of teachers and have watched their own parents balance teaching and parenting successfully. They probably enjoyed babysitting, teaching vacation Bible school, or working with children at summer camps. Is this you? If so, keep reading, because a love of children is an excellent reason to become a teacher.

Elementary teachers are qualified to teach all subject areas, but need to be exceptionally strong at teaching reading. Reading is the key to academic success, and literacy is stressed in every elementary school. An added bonus of being an elementary teacher is that you can change the grade levels you teach, and this gives you added job flexibility. For example, if you are a 2nd-grade teacher and your spouse gets relocated, you can teach any grade within your certification, usually kindergarten through 6th grade, depending on your state.

Of course, some of the biggest perks of teaching elementary school are the smiles and thank-you's you will receive from the children and their parents. Elementary teachers are appreciated!

MIDDLE GRADES TEACHERS

In order to teach students in the middle grades, you need to be a little like an elementary teacher and a little like a high school teacher. In other words, you need to like children/young adolescents, and you need to be a subject-matter specialist. And you need patience, lots of patience. Middle schoolers are at the awkward age, not children any more, and hardly young adults yet. They are testing themselves to see who they are and they will be testing you to see who you think they are. Sound complicated? Well, add the hormones of 12- to 14-year-olds to the mix and you now see the picture very clearly.

Why teach students in middle school? Because they are fun! They are filled with excitement, and they are at a very impressionable age. They are at a crossroads where their academic achievement can make them superstars or cause them to fall into the cracks. If you like fun and excitement and can laugh at almost anything, this may be the grade level for you.

HIGH SCHOOL TEACHERS

High school teachers consider themselves subject-matter experts and often report that they chose teaching because they love their subjects. High school teachers like to inspire teenagers/young adults to learn all there is to know about a subject. After all, for most high school students, this is the last chance they get at basic subjects. If they attend college they will study some general education courses, but will become immersed in their chosen field very quickly. Those who don't attend college will get most of their exposure to literature and great ideas from you—their high school teacher.

I became a high school teacher for the number one reason that research says I would—I loved my major subject, which was Spanish. I wanted all of my students to learn enough Spanish so that they could be interpreters at the United Nations, if they so desired. What a lofty goal! That's why people become teachers—to help the next generation have and achieve goals.

SPECIAL EDUCATION TEACHERS

One of the areas where new teachers are most needed is that of special education. These teachers choose one or more age levels with whom they will work and receive highly specialized training to be prepared to teach students with mental, emotional, or physical exceptionalities. Some teachers work in pull-out programs, providing help to remedial students or students with autism. Others work in the classroom with the regular teacher, but focus on the students with special learning or behavioral exceptionalities. Some special education teachers have their own classrooms and their own students all day.

So, what is the first step if you want to teach little, medium-sized, or almost-grown-up students? The first step is to untangle the maze of teacher certification so that you know what jobs are available to you.

TEACHER CERTIFICATION

What's the Easiest Way to Get Teacher Certification?

While there is no easy way to become a certified teacher, the clearest route is to earn teacher certification as an undergraduate student in an accredited program at a college or university. If you want to teach preschool-age children, major in early childhood education. To be an elementary teacher, major in elementary education. To be a middle school teacher, major in middle grades education. To be a high school teacher, you will most probably major in the subject you plan to teach, like math or English, and minor in teacher education. In a few large universities, you will choose to major in English education, as opposed to just English, if you want teacher certification.

It must be noted that every single state retains the right to set its teacher certification standards and to define the vocabulary. Some states refer to teacher certification as teacher licensure, and a teaching certificate as a teaching license. In this book the terms will be used interchangeably.

Since each state sets its own rules for certification, this means that the process of what to major in can vary from state to state. For example, to become a middle school teacher in one state, you major in middle grades education, but in the state next door, you major in your subject, minor in teacher education, and take some special courses for a middle school certificate. At one point, some states certified middle grades teachers who were elementary education majors and took extra classes about middle schools.

The certification process becomes even more complicated because early childhood, elementary, middle, and secondary have different definitions in different states. For example, in Georgia, early childhood education refers to a certificate to teach preschool through 5th grade. In other states, early childhood majors are certified to teach only preschool through kindergarten. Elementary education certification means kindergarten through 6th grade in many states, but not all. Middle grades certification may refer to grades 4 through 8 in some states, but only 6 through 8 in others. Even secondary certification is not the same in every state, as it can include grades 6 through 12, or grades 7 through 12, or just grades 9 through 12.

As you can imagine, special education certification is highly specialized and varies widely from state to state. In some states, special education teachers get certified as preschool, elementary, middle, or high school teachers and then add on courses for special education certification. In other states, they major in special education. Within the field of special education there are many areas, such as emotional/behavioral disorders, severe/profound, visually impaired, hearing impaired, and others. If this is your area of interest, check with your local university to find out the myriad of possibilities for special education certification.

So, even as a traditional undergraduate student, you must decide the general grade area that you want to teach—early childhood, elementary, middle school, or high school—and then choose the corresponding major at your college or university. Remember, too, that a state can change its certification levels at any time. Once certified, you are generally "grandfathered" against future changes, but not always. Each state also has rules about the continuing education course work you must pursue to keep your certificate. Continuing education may be offered by your school district or a regional office of education, free of charge. Some states may require actual course work at the university level to stay certified, even when you are teaching full time. Now you know what some teachers do with their summers!

When choosing an undergraduate program, make sure it is accredited by the state and meets all state certification requirements. Most states now require a teacher certification test, sometimes called a competency test, in addition to the completion of a teacher education program, in order to become fully certified. If this is the case, ask about your college's pass rates on the state test. A college with a high pass rate is probably doing a good job of preparing its education majors and minors—at least to pass the test. Consider this test to be similar to passing the bar exam after law school or the medical boards after med school.

To clarify, colleges and universities offer teacher education programs, which may be called teacher certification programs. In reality, it is the certification branch of the state government that ultimately grants a teaching license, or certification. For every state, the vocabulary varies. When a student completes an undergraduate program with teacher education, passes a state-mandated test, and clears any other hurdles, such as criminal background checks, then one is actually a fully certified, licensed teacher. Again, while this is not easy, knowing that you want to be a teacher when you begin college is the easiest way to earn teacher certification.

Since each state is different, see www.uky.edu/Education/TEP/usacert.html or www.professionalteacher.com for each state's minimum requirements. A college or university that is accredited by its state for teacher education will have a certification or advisement office that can tell you about the state's guidelines. In a college program, all of the rules and regulations about teacher certification should be explained in the first education course, Introduction to Education.

For those students who have already earned a bachelor's degree in a field, their choices of routes to teacher certification are quite varied.

1. Pursuing Undergraduate Course Work

With an earned bachelor's degree in any field, a student may return to college and take all the same courses that undergraduates are taking in the chosen education field. For example, the student majors in elementary education or middle grades education, or majors in mathematics with teacher certification, depending on the area in which he or she wants to teach. In some colleges, this earns teacher certification only, and the student is not a candidate for a second bachelor's degree. In other programs, this student would earn a second bachelor's degree. Some students like having a second bachelor's degree on their résumé; others don't want to "jump through the hoops" of general education requirements or specific graduation tests like they did as undergraduates the first time.

Whether to pursue the second bachelor's degree or just take the course work for a teaching certificate depends on the college's offerings, state requirements, and student choice. Some programs for teacher certification after the bachelor's degree is earned are referred to as "5th-year" programs.

2. Earning Teacher Certification Through Graduate Course Work

Students may enter a Master of Arts in Teaching (MAT) program to earn teacher certification. The course work is delivered at the graduate level, designed to meet the same requirements as undergraduate courses, but taught at a higher level. Many of these programs focus on significant field experiences in schools, in addition to stressing more theory than an undergraduate course might. New teachers with a master's degree start at higher salaries when hired by school districts.

Teacher certification can be earned in a Master of Education program. This differs from the MAT because students generally complete "regular" graduate courses in research and curriculum theory, perhaps including the writing of a master's-level thesis, in addition to graduate-level courses in "how to teach." These programs can be quite lengthy, a minimum of two to two-and-a-half years.

Another route in this category is to pursue teacher education courses as a graduate non-degree-seeking student. In some universities, this means that students with bachelor's degrees must be listed as graduate students, paying graduate tuition, but may be in undergraduate- or graduate-level courses that lead to teacher certification only, and no degree. For example, if the college's undergraduate courses are at the 100 to 400 levels, nondegree graduate courses are at the 500-level, with 600- or 700-level courses taught for those seeking graduate degrees.

3. Provisional Certification

In some states, teachers can begin teaching after having completed some teacher education courses, and then they may complete their teacher certification in the district where they teach, or through a nearby regional office of education. Regional offices of education have different names in different states and have traditionally been agencies that provided continuing education for practicing teachers and administrators to help them stay current in their fields. Staff developers tend to teach the district-level or regional office courses for certification. Obviously, these teachers are supposed to be monitored closely by mentors and administrators when hired without full certification or the benefits of student teaching.

Another variation of this route is when a teacher completes the remaining teacher certification courses at a college or university and is supervised by college or university personnel for a year before earning certification.

4. Test-Out Options

Some states are experimenting with test-out options to certify teachers provisionally. In Georgia, for example, teachers may begin teaching after passing a series of tests. They may teach up to five years once they enter the classroom. If they decide to remain in teaching, they then have to complete teacher certification by taking a minimum number of courses at the college or regional office of education level. They must be supervised in an internship at some time, as proof that they have the skills that a student teacher would have, if they choose to become fully certified.

5. Alternatives to Certification

There are some alternatives to certification that allow individuals with bachelor's degrees to begin teaching. One is a national program, Teach for America, that some states have replicated (see www.teachforamerica.org). The teachers in this program generally teach one to three years, unless they then decide to seek teacher certification. They are often assigned to very challenging classrooms in areas of the country where certified teachers cannot be recruited to teach.

6. Online/Distance Learning Programs

Online teacher certification programs may prove to be another way for those with a bachelor's degree to enter teaching, and more programs appear every year. For a clearinghouse of programs, see www.degree-site.com. Some online programs offer course work and then require practicum experience supervised by the sponsoring college/university. Distance learning courses can be an option in geographically isolated locations where small numbers of candidates make an off-campus course impractical.

The American Board for Certification of Teacher Excellence (ABCTE) offers online assessments for career changers who wish to be teachers. The website, www.abcte.org, explains which states, and which schools within those states, accept this type of online certification. The essential question to ask when looking at online or alternative certification is, "Will my state accept this certification for employment in its schools?"

7. The Community College Option

While a four-year degree remains a minimal standard for full teacher certification, some two-year colleges offer basic teacher education courses, such as Introduction to Education and Educational Psychology. Additionally, those with bachelor's degrees in fields unrelated to the area in which they wish to teach may choose to take general education courses or lower-level content courses at the community college because of lower tuition and availability of classes. The community college may become a more vital link in teacher education than ever before because of cost, accessibility, and convenience. Community college links to universities can be invaluable in combating the teacher shortage, for both traditional undergraduates and returning students.

Should I Start Teaching Before Earning Full Certification?

For undergraduate students, the only type of full-time teaching you can pursue before earning a bachelor's degree is substitute teaching, and, again, the rules for that vary for each state. Some undergraduates work as substitute teachers on spring break and in May, when the university is out, but the K–12 schools are still in session.

Some states do allow individuals with bachelor's degrees to begin teaching before becoming certified, if they meet the requirements discussed in the section on teacher certification. Just because people *can* do this, *should* they? Here are some questions to ask before jumping into the fire without certification.

First of all, would you like for your child to be in a classroom with a non–fully certified teacher? Would it bother you to know that some research indicates that teachers with less training have students with lower achievement scores? Will it bother you if other teachers resent you and treat you differently because you are teaching and earning your license at the same time? Will it offend you if these other teachers treat you in a negative manner rather than help you? Of course, you will be earning money rather than paying tuition to be a full-time student or student teacher, but you will be making less money than a certified teacher and you will be asked to teach the toughest classes and do the least pleasant extra duties.

Challenges of Earning Certification While Teaching

Ask teachers about their jobs and they will relate challenges. Today's students are indeed very diverse — in academic backgrounds, social experiences, socio-economic levels, language, and motivation. The "best" jobs probably have a long list of certified teachers applying for openings. Often, non–fully certified teachers must take on the most challenging teaching positions. Be prepared to deal with more student challenges than would be the norm in other classrooms, including special education, language minority, and remedial students.

Not knowing the specialized vocabulary of the teaching profession and not knowing the routines of a particular school district will mean a high learning curve during the first few months on the job. Hopefully, you will be assigned a mentor teacher who can "show you the ropes" and help you stay ahead of deadlines. Take advantage of all professional development opportunities and be receptive to ideas from colleagues, supervisors, and instructors of the courses you take.

Yes, being a new teacher is like being a new employee in any field in some respects, but it is unlike other jobs because you are onstage doing your work in front of 25 to 35 students at a time. The principal expects you to do the same job of a veteran teacher from day one, and that includes not only managing student behavior, but also getting students to learn enough material to pass end-of-the-year tests! Your success will be evaluated by the scores your students earn on tests. You convinced your employer that you could teach while earning certification, so you have to prove yourself to the employer, the students, the parents, and even your colleagues. New teachers sometimes report that they do not get all the help and support they need, and non–fully certified teachers may encounter resentment or negativity on the part of some colleagues. Your district may be required to inform parents of your certification status, and this may cause some difficult phone calls or complaint letters from parents. However, in some districts, if only the fully certified teachers were teaching and non–fully certified personnel weren't hired, the class sizes would be astronomically high. Remember that you were needed or you wouldn't have been hired.

So why do people choose this route? For many, being a full-time student for two years is simply an impossible situation financially, and teaching while earning certification is the only option. Sometimes employers encourage substitute teachers or parents who participate actively in the schools to start teaching full time. If you do make this choice, talk to others who have done so before you. It can be terribly frustrating to be a new teacher all day, a student at night, and then to balance all of life's other responsibilities—home, children, spouse, and so forth. The stress level for all new teachers is high, but it is really high for those who are taking the course work simultaneously. Imagine how much easier it would be if you could do one thing at a time—learn to teach, practice your skills in student teaching, then get a job.

Teaching Out of State

Since your teaching certification/license is only good in the state where it is earned, what happens when you need or want to move? Well, the first thing to do is to go to the Internet and read about the state where you intend to move. See www.uky.edu/Education/TEP/usacert.html or www.professional teacher.com. Either site will lead you to the information about teacher certification for each state. You can also use any search engine, such as google.com, and type in teacher certification and the name of the state. If the information isn't completely clear, you will at least have the basic information and contact sources for your specific questions.

Some states have reciprocity agreements, which means that they basically accept another state's certification, provided it is *full* certification and not provisional or alternative. If that is the case, you simply fill out paperwork, pay a fee, and you may be eligible to begin teaching. If your current state and the new state where you seek to teach do not have reciprocity agreements, then the process may include some course work and testing. Some states require a transcript evaluation to determine if you have had the minimum number of hours of course work in general education and teacher education. Some states have stricter requirements than others about the number of special education courses that must be taken. I know of one case where a fully certified elementary teacher moved and had to take a government course and a foreign language course in the new state to be fully certified. In another case, a teacher with full certification and several years of experience had to take a speech communication course!

In most cases, you may begin teaching in the new state while completing the course work or testing if you were fully certified in the first state. Again, knowing this information may help career changers who already have a bachelor's degree as they choose their route to teacher certification.

The hardest way to get certification is to move out of state before finishing teacher certification in one state. In the past, many students decided to finish bachelor's degrees and go ahead and graduate without student teaching, perhaps because that saved them a semester in college. If a person does not student teach, or skips even one class in a teacher education program, they don't get certified. When moving to another state with a bachelor's degree, the teacher education course work, but no student teaching, a student probably finds himself looking at another three semesters or more to finish. Why? Because in the new state, a person can't just go to a college and student teach there. Colleges and universities usually require a minimum number of hours in *their* program before they place a student teacher, and that minimum is usually two semesters of work.

So, the old adage about getting your teaching credentials as a backup plan is still true. If you think that you might ever want to teach, get the teacher certification where you are. Moving to another state in the middle of a program, or even near the end, will add significant work to your completion deadline.

Why do people want to teach out of state? Sometimes, it's where the jobs are! Sometimes, it's where your spouse's job is, and since teaching is considered the family-friendly profession, you are still more likely than some other professionals to find a similar job in another state. Teachers are needed in all the states, and with a little persistence, you can get certified out of state.

No Child Left Behind and What It Means for Teacher Certification

In January of 2002, George W. Bush signed the No Child Left Behind Act, which was intended to improve student achievement, close achievement gaps, and make teacher quality a high priority (U.S. Department of Education, 2004, and www.ed.gov/nclb/landing.jhtml). This legislation "outlines the minimum qualifications needed by teachers: a bachelor's degree, full state certification and demonstration of subject-matter competency for each subject taught" (U.S. Department of Education, 2004, p. 3). However, each state retains the right to define full state certification. Provisionally and emergency-certified teachers can still begin teaching under NCLB, as long as they meet their state's guidelines.

One of the largest debates stimulated by the NCLB legislation is that of the "highly qualified" teacher. Just what defines a highly qualified teacher? In simple terms, imagine yourself as a parent. What do you want your child's teacher to know and be able to do? What would make you request one teacher over another if you could choose your child's teacher? What results do you expect your child's teacher to accomplish with your child? Can he or she accomplish those same results with every child in the room (hence, leaving no child behind)?

If it is true that "teachers are one of the most critical factors in how well students achieve" (U.S. Department of Education, 2004, p. 9), then logic dictates that the more qualified a teacher is, the more students will achieve. NCLB capitalizes on this logic and stresses subject-matter competency for teachers of all grades and subjects. This subject-matter competency must be demonstrated in each core subject that the teacher teaches. Most states have chosen to use standardized tests as the measure of subject-matter competency of the teacher. Therefore, students in education programs must complete course work, earn certification, and pass state tests in the subjects they teach to be considered highly qualified (see, for example, www.teacherquality.us). Colleges and universities have changed their programs to ensure that their graduates who receive full teacher certification have met the highly qualified mandate of NCLB.

One final mandate of the No Child Left Behind legislation is that of parent notification with regard to schools and teachers. Beginning in school year 2002–2003, states had to produce report cards that included information on student performance, graduation rates, and the professional qualifications of teachers. Districts must report the same information—and that information must be broken down to the school level. Therefore, parents must be informed of the certification status of their child's teacher—whether that teacher is fully certified, or teaching on an emergency certificate. Some districts are meeting this mandate by sending letters home to parents about the credentials of their child's teacher—especially when the teacher is not yet fully certified. Imagine the chaos this may create in some communities! These letters must be carefully worded, and teachers who are earning certification while teaching full time need supportive administrators to help them deal with potentially upset parents.

Special Requirements to Be a Certified Teacher Today

Teachers work in the public eye. That means that they are certainly held to a high standard with regard to ethics and conduct. Some would say that they are held to a higher standard than those in some other professions. Because of the public's demand for high-quality teachers, as evidenced by NCLB, most states have some special requirements for teachers that would not be asked of individuals in other jobs. Some states ask candidates to sign a code of conduct or ethical code when they apply for their first teaching certificate. If an applicant has a felony record, or even a series of DUI offenses, this may keep the applicant from being granted a teaching certificate.

Applicants for teaching certificates must list their criminal records, even for offenses such as shoplifting, and the state will determine if the applicant qualifies to teach. Remember, this is after the applicant has completed a bachelor's degree and the teacher education program and passed the competency tests! If a student has any question about whether his or her past offenses will keep them from earning a certificate, the time to ask is before doing all the course work, student teaching, and taking the final high-stakes certification test. In most teacher education programs, students are made aware of the state's code of conduct and ethical clauses early in the program, probably in the Education 101 class. Most teacher education programs are so rigorous that they make the state's final requirements their own entrance requirements to a program, and do a criminal background check on students before they enter the final stages of the program. Criminal background checks and fingerprinting are generally required by all states for new teachers, and are increasingly required of candidates in teacher education programs before they ever set foot in a school for a field experience or student teaching.

Have the states gone overboard in requiring teachers to have such background checks? After all, aren't teachers professionals and shouldn't they be accorded due respect for their professional status? The answers to these questions are always debatable. You might want to ask yourself, What kind of person do I want teaching my children for seven hours a day? Would I be concerned if a person with a string of felonies decided to teach? There are always at least two sides to every story. What's the job market like if schools are resorting to hiring people with criminal backgrounds anyway?

THE JOB MARKET FOR PRESCHOOL TO 12TH-GRADE TEACHERS

It would be hard to pick up any newspaper or news magazine in September and not read about the teacher shortage, teacher quality, the status of schools, or the job of a teacher. The public does indeed have a lot of interest in their schools, and a teacher reports to many bosses—the students, the parents, the school administration, and the community.

Is there really a shortage of teachers? The American Association for Employment in Education (AAEE), tracks the supply and demand of teachers on an annual basis, and reports shortages of teachers in certain fields. In 2006, AAEE reported considerable shortages of special education teachers, as well as mathematics teachers. There were some shortages reported for the many fields of science—chemistry, physics, and biology among them; and for English as a second language (ESOL), bilingual education, and Spanish. The AAEE report indicated some surplus in elementary education, health, physical education, and social studies. Those in education recognize that the shortages of teachers in special education, mathematics, sciences, Spanish, and bilingual and ESOL have existed for some time.

Where are new teachers needed? They are needed in the parts of the country where populations continue to grow. The sunbelt needs teachers because people with children migrate there and school-age populations are growing in Arizona, Florida, Nevada, and Texas. Suburban areas of big cities need teachers because that's where there is growth—suburban Atlanta is a prime example, or suburban Phoenix. Of course, many schools that are considered "inner-city" urban ones need teachers because of high employee turnover and low teacher retention.

Some researchers contend that colleges are preparing enough teachers, but the shortages exist because of the low retention rates of those hired (Ingersoll, 2003). Breaux and Wong (2003) write that "between 40 and 50 percent will leave during the first seven years of their career, and more than two-thirds of those will do so in the first four years of teaching" (p. 3). The estimates of those teachers who leave the profession because of urban and other difficult placements are even higher.

Some teacher shortages are real, because of the numbers of teachers who are retiring, the numbers who are quitting, and because of the growing numbers of students with special needs, both in special education and language acquisition.

INCREASE YOUR MARKETABILITY

What does all of this mean to a job seeker? If you want to ensure getting a job, major in a high-needs field, like special education, mathematics, science, ESOL, bilingual education, or Spanish. If these fields are not your interest, then you may want to increase your marketability by adding as many special education, ESOL, or Spanish classes as possible to your college program. A fully certified elementary teacher who took four years of Spanish in high school, two years of Spanish in college, and studied abroad in Costa Rica one summer, stands out to a recruiter who needs a teacher with some knowledge of Spanish for a 2nd-grade position. Elementary teachers who are willing to work in after-school programs or teach enrichment classes over breaks are also more apt to be hired. Of course, a longer teaching day and working on vacation make for a more tedious first year of teaching, too.

Teachers of social studies, health, and physical education have long known that coaching may be the key to getting their first job, since there are actually surpluses of teachers in these fields. If coaching is what you want to do, then advertise it in your cover letter and résumé, and be ready to spend the hours it takes to coach a winning team.

Adding a reading endorsement to your certification makes you more employable, especially in a middle school. So may adding an endorsement to teach gifted children. An endorsement is an addition to your initial teaching certificate that allows you to teach in that field. While the coursework varies for endorsements, some can be earned with only three or four college courses. Some students add endorsements before graduation, while others take graduate courses to do so. In many states, an endorsement can also be earned by taking seminars and short courses that are offered by a regional office of education. Once the coursework or seminars are complete, you must apply for the endorsement by completing the appropriate paperwork with your state teacher certification office. Sometimes the paperwork can be done at your college, university, or school district.

Employers like to hire certified teachers with endorsements because they can use these teachers to teach a few classes a day or to work with special populations of students (e.g., English-language learners, special education students, remedial readers) in their own classroom, saving the district the cost of hiring yet another teacher. It also helps a teacher who has more skills to employ when charged with teaching these students.

Some high school teachers also volunteer to produce plays or yearbooks, sponsor the cheerleaders, or coach the scholastic bowl in order to get their first jobs. In order to do one of these things, you should have some background and experience with the extracurricular duty, either in high school or college. Volunteering to coach gymnastics if you've never even done gymnastics could prove disastrous. Again, some states place requirements on the coaches and sponsors, such as an endorsement to coach or first aid training, before you can work with students in extra duties.

How else can you increase the likelihood of getting a job? Good grades help you to stand out, since recruiters know that high grades are associated with high class attendance, and an employer wants you to attend school every day as the teacher. Good recommendations from professors, your student teaching supervising teacher, and former employers are a must. Being willing to move to a part of the country that needs teachers makes you more employable, and working a few years in a challenging job may help you secure a second teaching job later. Your interpersonal and communication skills and the ability to interview well will help you to earn a job. Simply knowing how to job search, how to create the necessary paperwork, and how to interview will help you get a teaching job. These skills are all taught in upcoming chapters of this book.

BEING A SUBSTITUTE TEACHER

Do you remember how you and your classmates treated the substitute teachers? Now, do you want to be one? Why would anyone choose to enter teaching through this route? First of all, being a substitute teacher remains a tried-and-true way to get your foot in the door for a full-time teaching job. If you work as a substitute and are successful at it, the principal notices and your name comes to the top of the list when you apply for a position.

Substituting is a good way for "placebound" job candidates to get jobs. A placebound candidate is someone who cannot leave a certain geographic area because of the spouse's job or other family obligations. A placebound candidate can't search for any available high school position in English in a four-state radius, but must work within commuting distance of his or her personal responsibilities. If you must work in, or if you want to work in, a certain district, then you may have to substitute teach, and do an exemplary job at it, until an opening in your field occurs.

Substitutes are usually in demand, especially in the spring semester. Some traditional undergraduate students work as substitutes when the school year at the university is over so that they have more experience on their résumés. Some adult career changers start working as substitutes in order to decide if they really want to become teachers, and to get experience as well. Of course, most substitute teachers do it for the money, which is considerably above minimum wage and allows you to be done with your work by three or four in the afternoon. The hours of a substitute teacher are compatible with the hours of your own children's school, so you can pick them up and be their caregiver. The hours also allow you to take graduate courses in teacher education, most of which are at night.

How Do I Get a Job Subbing?

Remember the section of this book on teacher certification? Well, each state has its own rules for the certification of substitute teachers, as well, and the same variance from state to state is true. Some states require only a high school diploma and training by the local school district to earn a substitute teaching certificate. Other states seek substitutes with a minimum of an associate's or bachelor's degree. Generally, fully certified teachers are paid a higher daily rate as substitutes than are others who are not certified teachers.

And yes, in areas with large universities and a surplus of teachers, there will be a larger pool of substitutes who are already fully certified teachers. Districts will hire them first, but don't give up and you will probably get calls to work once you complete the paperwork, get a substitute certificate, attend the district training, and pass the criminal background check.

You can start at the state's department of education website for basic information, and then find the websites for the districts in your area where you intend to apply for work. (Use www.uky.edu/Education/TEP/usacert.html or www.professionalteacher.com to get started, or type in the name of the district.) Almost all school districts have a website with information about how to apply to be a substitute teacher, and if openings are available. If there is no website, go to the yellow pages and look up the phone number of the director of human resources for the district. Call and ask for information about substitute certification and an application for that district.

The secret to getting a job is to then do exactly what the website or human resources director says to do! If there are deadlines, meet them. If there is required training, take it. If there is optional training, attend. If there is a handbook to read, read it. If a résumé and cover letter are required, send them in. If you are using substitute teaching to get a job, then you have to put your best foot forward from the very first contact. Some substitutes are *never* hired as full-time teachers because the district personnel office knows that their paperwork will always be late and that their questions will always be ones that were already answered in a training session. Don't let this be you.

Surviving at Substitute Teaching

The motto of the substitute teacher who not only survives, but thrives, is "be prepared." Don't start subbing without any background on classroom management and discipline, or without any knowledge of the school and district. Do your homework about the district by reading their website, talking with teachers (especially other subs), and attending their workshops once you are in the substitute pool. If limited training is available, do the reading and research on your own. No one should sub unless they have read at least one book on classroom management/discipline and one on how to be a substitute teacher. See the books and websites listed in the bibliography of this book, and start doing your homework.

A Dozen Things to Do Before Starting a Job as a Substitute Teacher

1. Read and study about classroom management and discipline.
2. Read the district and school handbooks and know their policies.

3. Find out where to park and know a school support staff/secretary's contact phone number.
4. Always introduce yourself in the main office and learn the names of the administrators and office support staff.
5. Dress professionally. No jeans or casual clothes. Gentlemen should wear khakis, shirt, and tie. Ladies should wear dress slacks, conservative skirts, dresses, or jumpers. Be neat and well groomed.
6. Prepare a survival kit with age-appropriate books to read to students, word puzzles, and other time-filling activities. Also pack basic school supplies, like paper, pencil, scissors, tape, and so forth.
7. Pack a sack lunch—you never know what will be served in the cafeteria or if you will have time to eat it.
8. Bring lots of note cards that can be used by the students to make name cards for their desks. When you leave, take the name cards with you and keep them in a file in case you are called back to the class. This helps you to know students' names immediately and gives students something to do while you are getting organized in the room.
9. Always write a short report for the regular teacher, including what you accomplished, which pages were covered, what homework was actually assigned, and so forth.
10. Thank all administrators and support staff as you leave.
11. Help your family understand that this is real work, and that you are *not* to be called during the day. Teachers can't usually take calls anyway, except in cases of real emergency.
12. Use what little spare time there is to talk with other teachers and "network." After all, many teachers get to request their substitute when they know in advance that they will be gone.

TEACHING IN PRIVATE SCHOOLS AND IN HIGHER EDUCATION

As a senior in an education program, or as a job seeker who is changing careers, you may have asked yourself, "Should I consider teaching jobs in private schools or in higher education?" The answer to this question is, "It all depends." Teaching in private schools can be somewhat similar to teaching in the public systems, but there can also be big differences.

Comparison of Elements of Public and Private Preschool–12th-Grade Teaching

(Hint: These are good things to find out before accepting *any* teaching job.)

1. Salary—Private schools tend to pay less. In some cases the pay is considerably less, where in other geographic areas it may be similar. Consider the whole benefit package as well as salary. The retirement packages and health and life insurance benefits of state school systems are generally tough to beat.
2. Teaching assignments—Private schools tend to have smaller class sizes, because they are appealing to parents who want individualized attention for their children. The difference between teaching 28 third graders in a public setting versus 12 in a private one may make you rethink the salary difference. However, with small class sizes at the private secondary schools, you may end up teaching six classes a day with six separate lesson preparations. In a big public school, your assignment might be six classes a day with only one lesson preparation. For example, six classes of first-year Spanish, as opposed to one class of first-year Spanish, one class each of second-, third-, and fourth-year Spanish, and two French classes at a private school.
3. Paperwork and adherence to state mandates—Some private schools create their own curricula and allow tremendous flexibility for their teachers. For some teachers, who hate being tied to state-mandated curricula and testing, this can be a blessing. However, parents who pay private school tuition tend to want even *better* academic results than the public schools are providing, so be ready for parents to insist that their children be tested and that their scores be significantly higher when the results are tallied.
4. Certification—Some private schools do not require their teachers to have state teacher certification. This means that you can teach in a private school and go to school at night to earn your certification. The opposite side of this coin is that parents who pay tuition want their private schools to be accredited, and this means that more and more will require fully certified teachers. Full certification also helps you to get the job at the private school in the first place, where there may be many applicants for a good position.
5. Tuition breaks for your children—Many teachers take private school jobs so that their own children can attend the school. This is true of preschool through high school levels.
6. Discipline problems and academic diversity—Some teachers insist that teaching at a private school has kept them sane because there are fewer discipline issues and less academic diversity. Private schools do not have to put up with discipline problems. They can just kick students out and send them back to public schools. Some private schools require a certain grade point average and recommendations for admission, so

when a teacher is assigned a 9th-grade English class to teach, the students are at 9th-grade reading levels or above. What a joy! As with every argument, there is a second side to this one, too. Some private schools accept students whose parents feel that the public school isn't catering to their child's special needs (behavioral or academic) and pay big bucks for extra attention. If this is the philosophy of the school, your private school classes may be populated with some very "high-maintenance" students.

7. Philosophy of education—This one may be the biggest one to consider. If you want to teach science from a creationist point of view, then you need to choose a private school that endorses that philosophy. If you want to lead children in prayer and feel that it is the school's job to build a child's character in a certain mold, then you need to be in a private school that holds the same values as your philosophy. The separation of church and state remains strongly intact in public schools.

To summarize the decision-making process about private vs. public school teaching, you have to know the philosophy of the private school and ask a lot of questions in the interview. Some private schools still require new teachers to live in the dorms and serve as dorm parents. If that sounds like fun to you, and the free lodging appeals to your frugality, consider the job. If that sounds like torture to you, don't do it! Why do some new teachers take private school jobs? Because it's the best, or only, job opportunity in their geographic area. Don't rule out private school teaching, but always find out the hidden duties. In other words, read the fine print!

COMMUNITY COLLEGE TEACHING OPTIONS

The growth of community colleges in the United States in the last 50 years has been astounding. These institutions serve many needs, from offering remedial education courses to supplying students with a full two years of college-level general education. Their low tuition and easy accessibility have made them favorites of traditional and nontraditional students.

So, how do you get a job at a community college? Many community college instructors are veteran high school teachers who earn their full-time community college jobs after teaching part time at night for the college for several years. Other instructors are actually PhD's who choose to teach at the community college level because of the lowered expectations about research and writing there. Most community college instructors hold at least a master's degree, and many hold PhD's or are working at completing them. Do community college instructors need to be state-certified teachers? No. They are generally hired on the basis of their subject-matter expertise.

To look at the community college job market, read the *Chronicle of Higher Education,* which can be found online at chronicle.com. Since most community colleges are state institutions, the pay and benefits are generally quite good. Without a doctorate, the pay would be very similar to teaching at a public K–12 school, but your schedule would be different. You would most likely teach approximately 12 to 15 contact hours per week at a community college, as opposed to 30 contact hours a week in a high school. A contact hour is when you are actually in front of the class teaching. Your students would be paying tuition, and the classroom climate is different than that of high school teaching.

WHAT ABOUT COLLEGE/UNIVERSITY TEACHING?

Teaching in the ivory towers of higher education looks particularly appealing to many people. They see the hours as wonderful and the task of teaching genuinely interested students as a pleasure. While you do not need teacher certification to teach at the four-year college level, you do need a doctorate in your field. Everyone probably knows someone who teaches full time at a college with only a master's degree, but these people are considered adjuncts or lecturers and have much lower pay than tenure-track professors.

To become a professor, most people enter doctoral programs after earning their master's degrees and work as teaching assistants while doing so. A doctoral program generally takes three to five years after a master's, depending on the speed with which one researches and writes one's thesis.

In the field of teacher education, professors who teach people to be teachers have generally been successful classroom teachers for several years before entering higher education. Some K–12 teachers earn their advanced degrees while teaching full time, attending night and summer school graduate courses. In the field of teacher education, as well as the general humanities (English, history, social sciences), beginning college professors make less than high school teachers with similar education and several years of experience, although there is great disparity in salaries in higher education, with some salaries being quite high. Each professor often negotiates on his or her own for salaries, unless the university has a faculty union. High salaries go to those professors with great reputations and strong publication records. The biggest difference about teaching in higher education is the publishing factor. Professors must research, write, and get published in their fields. Everyone who job searches in higher education reads the *Chronicle of Higher Education* (chronicle.com).

AND YOU MIGHT WANT TO CONSIDER ADMINISTRATION

Some people leave teaching, but stay in education by becoming administrators. The route for doing this is to be a successful classroom teacher, usually with a minimum of three years of experience, and to earn at least a master's degree and the state's certification in administration/school leadership. There are some alternative routes to administration. Again, one has to go by each state's rules and guidelines.

Everyone knows about principals and superintendents, because we all went to school and know that the principal runs the individual school and the superintendent runs the whole district. Principals and superintendents earn salaries that are much higher than teachers. In fact, most principals' salaries are double that of the average salary of a classroom teacher, and superintendents generally make above six figures.

If running the show and shouldering so much responsibility does not appeal to you, there are other levels of responsibility for administrators. Curriculum directors are generally paid as assistant principals or assistant superintendents, and they work with teachers with regard to what should be taught. They help to select textbooks and guide the school to meet the state-mandated curriculum. Instead of teaching children, they teach professional development classes for the teachers. Personnel directors recruit and hire new teachers, and generally plan their induction, mentoring, and support. Assistant principals help with all areas of running the school, and generally spend quite a lot of time working with discipline. Assistant superintendents are generally specialized—one for budget, one for personnel, one for curriculum, and so forth. There are lots of opportunities in school administration. Is there a downside? Politics and public relations play very important roles in any administrator's job. Administrators must be advocates for students and teachers, while making parents and the community happy. It's no small task.

TO CONSIDER

1. If you are completing a program in teacher education, what can you still do before starting your job search to enhance your marketability?
2. Write down your personal list of reasons for becoming a teacher and then write out the reasons you have decided to teach at your chosen grade level/subject.
3. Pick a state where you might want to move, and find out about their teacher certification requirements.

4. Why might you choose to work as a substitute teacher? What are the rules for substitute teaching in your state?
5. Go online and research everything you can find about two different districts in which you would like to teach. If each district were to offer you a job, which might you consider?
6. Where do you see yourself in five years? Ten years? Would your career path lead to a community college or university teaching job? Have you considered school administration?

2

Your Job Search

Now that you know all that there is to know about becoming a teacher, it's time to talk about the job search. How do candidates actually go about finding the job openings and winning a chance at a job interview? In the field of teaching, you don't just go out to schools with your résumé in hand, and the local newspaper want ads rarely list teaching jobs. The search for teaching jobs begins at your university, with online searching and career fairs being key components in the process.

THE TRADITIONAL SEARCH STARTS WITH THE COLLEGE/UNIVERSITY

Two offices within your college or university can help you find out where the jobs are. One is the student teaching office or the certification office within the department of education. Oftentimes, schools will call one of these offices and ask them to advertise their job fairs and their teacher openings. School administrators and personnel directors feel that they have a good working relationship with the student teaching or certification office because they host so many student teachers and practicum students. Do not rely upon the student teaching office to help you find a job, however, as this is not the main function of the office. Many times the student teaching office does nothing except put flyers about jobs on a bulletin board in the hallway.

The second office that can help you find a job is actually the most important—the college career center. Many career centers will offer specialized seminars just for teacher education majors and will teach you how to write a cover letter and résumé that are customized for a job search in education.

The Credentials File

A service that career centers often maintain just for teacher candidates is that of the credentials files. In a tight job market, an education major may send out dozens of résumés and cover letters to net a job. You cannot ask your professors and your cooperating teacher to write a letter to *each* district where you apply, but you can have each writer of your letters of recommendation send one letter to the career center. The career center then puts copies of the three to five letters that are written on your behalf in a neat file, and this file can be mailed to as many potential employers as you request. The credentials file adds professionalism to your application package to a school district. Some career centers add a page about the college's teacher education program, noting the college's accreditations and other highlights, making the credentials file even more important. Some colleges have made this service an online one, and more will in the future.

In addition to the credentials file service, the career center is the clearinghouse for employers who seek to hire new teachers. The districts that need teachers send their openings to the career center for posting. The postings may still be on paper on a bulletin board, but are generally online now. During the last semester of your teacher education program, read the career center's job postings regularly. If you want a job that starts in August, you need to start searching seriously in January.

The postings in your career center may be helpful in locating openings in your field, but the career center's teacher job fair will probably net you even more contacts in a short amount of time. You may attend a job fair the semester or year before you are actually on the job market if you want to see what happens at one firsthand. Volunteer to be a worker when you are a junior and then you will be more comfortable attending as a senior. Volunteers do everything from serve coffee to carry boxes for recruiters. They get a behind-the-scenes view of the whole job fair. Consider the following scenario.

A recruiter who arrived late to a job fair found herself struggling with her briefcase and a large box of pamphlets as she approached the door to the college gymnasium. Much to her surprise, the student who entered the gym immediately before her did not stop and hold the door for her. Later that afternoon, the student was one of her scheduled interviewees. Needless to say, he or she did not get a job offer or an offer for an on-site interview. The moral to this story: good manners and being nice always count. Also, past behavior is the best predictor of future performance, and teachers have to be helpful, team players.

Once you are ready for the job market (in the last semester of your program), be sure to attend the job fair as a candidate. The career center should provide orientation for getting the most from the specific fair; see the section later in this chapter on how to prepare for a job fair, as well.

What the Career Center Can Do for Alumni Seeking Teaching Jobs

Most seniors know how much the career center can help them in their job search. Those who return to the university to pursue teacher certification, with or without a degree, may not realize that they too are eligible for the services of the career center. If you are a student at any level—undergraduate, graduate, or part-time—use all of the services offered by the university where you are a student. You have paid for these services with your tuition.

A growing area of service from the career center is for alumni who seek help with career changes. This may be you as a teacher candidate. First of all, you may want to return to your career center for job counseling advice on how to become a certified teacher, or a recertified one, if you've let your license lapse. If recently certified through another institution, you may even go back to your alma mater for help with the teacher job search, in addition to using the center at the college where you took teacher certification classes. Fully certified teachers who lose jobs due to budget cuts, or who need to job search in other districts in the area should take advantage of their home institution's career center and its job fairs, as well. As an alum, the career center can help you with polishing your résumé and cover letter, job searching online, and preparing to participate in a job fair. Always do the preplanning with the career center, and don't just show up at a job fair expecting to be admitted, as candidates generally need to register and may be required to have a credentials file in order to participate at any seminar or job fair.

ONLINE JOB SEARCHES

In addition to the college career center's online job postings, there are other common online sites that teacher candidates need to become familiar with: district sites, state sites, national/international ones, and ones sponsored by professional organizations. Always read the fine print and be aware that some commercial sites will charge fees.

Why should you use an individual district site in your job search? Once a candidate has heard of an opening, either formally or informally, he or she needs to learn everything about the district. The minimum that you need to know is what is on the website. Many sites include student demographic information, test scores, awards, teacher salaries, and information about the community. Asking questions in an interview about basic information that is on the website indicates that you don't do your homework! Who wants a teacher who doesn't prepare? If you are placebound and cannot move for a job to a district outside of where you live, then you need to read the district site for job openings regularly.

How do you find the district sites? One way is to type in the full name of the district on google.com or another search engine. A second way is to go to the district site from the state's website.

One caution about district websites: a website is only as good as the people who put the information on it. Some sites are not updated regularly. Others may not post openings for teachers, just for noncertified personnel, such as cooks and bus drivers. Read the site carefully and compare its openings to those on the state's website.

State Websites

The department of education in each state will have a website. It was the starting place for your search on teacher certification rules and guidelines. Now that you are actually job searching, go back to the state's site and look for a link to job openings. If you don't have your state department of education site bookmarked, do a search for department of education and your state name, then bookmark it. If the state's department of education doesn't net you the state's job openings, then type in teacher jobs and the name of your state. You can also use the American Association for Employment in Education's *Job Search Handbook for Educators* for a list of sites for all 50 states. See their website at www.aaee.org. Sample statewide job websites include:

- www.arizonaeducationjobs.com
- www.calteach.com
- www.teachinflorida.com
- www.teachgeorgia.org
- www.iowaeducationjobs.com
- www.tea.state.tx.us

Some websites are more user-friendly than others. Other cautions and benefits about these sites include:

1. Some states may require every district to post every job opening on the site, while other states do not require this. Hence, there may be jobs in the state that are not posted. You have to dig deeper for them, perhaps on the district's site or by reading the postings at your career center.

2. Some districts may require you to register on the state website *before* they will consider your application at the district level. Again, find out from reading the websites if this requirement exists.
3. Some state sites may have outdated information.
4. State sites may serve as recruitment sites, providing information about cost of living, housing, and so forth. Use this information to help you decide if moving out of state is for you. Some state sites may paint a rosy picture of teaching there, if they are indeed recruiting. Read the fine print and gather information from other sources as well.
5. Some state sites will provide a direct link to the district site, which will provide much more information about a specific job. Read that information before applying. If a state site has specific rules about applying to a district online, follow those rules.

National/International Sites and Commercial Sites

A quick online search for "teaching jobs" will net many responses. The following are examples of national sites that purport to match teacher candidates to job openings around the country, and in some cases, around the world:

- www.teachers-teachers.com
- jobs.teachers.net
- www.k12jobs.com
- www.teaching-jobs.org
- www.abcteachingjobs.com

How do these sites work? Generally, school districts that need to hire teachers will pay to post their job openings on the site. Candidates can use the site for free. Some of the sites, such as teachers-teachers.com, assist the candidate with résumé and cover letter writing, providing a tutorial on how to do these things. On many of these sites, the candidate must register (still free), and will then be able to get individual jobs in their field e-mailed to them, either directly or to a page that is created for them on the site. It's a lot like how the airlines let the consumer keep track of their own frequent flyer miles.

The upside of a commercial site is that it can provide you with information about thousands of job openings in your field. You may want to read a couple of these sites on a daily basis as you job search, to see what openings there are in your field. If you are free to move, you can job search in any state at the click of a mouse. The sites help you have an online résumé and cover letter and often provide other job search information and advice.

The downside is that employers are charged to use these sites, so the only jobs listed are the ones from districts that know about and pay to use the site. If you use only a dot-com site, you might miss a job opening that is 20 minutes away from your apartment. The best advice about online searching is to use a combination of sites that meet your needs. Compare the openings listed on three or four of the commercial sites with the ones listed on state sites where you are interested in teaching, then narrow your search by looking at the individual districts. If you are starting to think that this part of the job search may take some time and work, you are right! But imagine how difficult it was to search when we didn't have the Internet for all of this good information.

When you do find a job that interests you on a site, follow the directions for applying for it according to the site—each commercial site is a little bit different. On some, you will respond electronically only, by submitting your online résumé and cover letter that were created specifically for that one site. For other sites, you may be directed to e-mail a district directly, and then send paperwork accordingly.

Employment Opportunities Provided on Sites of Professional Organizations

As a new teacher, you should definitely be aware of the national professional organizations, which are sometimes called specialized professional associations (SPAs). In your teacher education program you first became aware of these organizations because they create general standards for the curriculum. In other words, these are the organizations that create the guidelines for what is taught in the schools. If you are an elementary teacher, you will need to know about and use several different organizations, as elementary teachers teach everything. Middle and high school teachers will use the organizations that specialize in their subject fields. Now you can go to the websites of the organizations that best fit your field and see if they list employment opportunities of interest to you. Some examples follow:

- The International Reading Association (IRA) at www.reading.org
- The National Council of Teachers of English (NCTE) at www.ncte.org
- The National Science Teachers Association (NSTA) at www.nsta.org
- The National Council of Teachers of Mathematics (NCTM) at www.nctm.org
- The National Council for the Social Studies (NCSS) at www.ncss.org
- The American Council on the Teaching of Foreign Languages (ACTFL) at www.actfl.org

- Special education—The Council for Exceptional Children (CEC) at www.cec.sped.org
- The International Technology Education Association (ITEA) at www.iteaconnect.org

Unlike the commercial sites, you won't be able to create a personal home-page on one of the sites of the professional organizations, but many do post openings. If you find an opening, then read about the district that has posted it, and apply as directed. The upside of applying for a job found on the web-site of a professional organization is that you will tell the employer in your cover letter where you found the opening, and they will know you read the website to remain updated on the profession!

Other Professional Organizations

In addition to the specialized professional associations listed above, there are also national professional organizations in education, and reading their web-sites may provide you with resources for your job search. Try the following:

- Kappa Delta Pi at www.kdp.org
- Phi Delta Kappa at www.pdkintl.org
- The National Education Association at www.nea.org
- The American Federation of Teachers at www.aft.org

The professional associations, both specialized and general, have national conferences. Attending a national conference may open doors for you to em-ployers, who sometimes recruit at these events. Even if the national conference doesn't feature recruiters, it remains an excellent way to network with practic-ing teachers, and sometimes word-of-mouth is the way candidates find jobs.

NETWORKING AND WORD-OF-MOUTH JOB OPENINGS

While no candidate should rely upon hearing about a job opening as his or her only method of job searching, we all know that hearing about local jobs is still a viable means of finding the right job opening for you. Rather than consid-ering word-of-mouth or gossip as a means to job search, let's call this tech-nique networking.

If you are student teaching during the last semester of your teacher education program, you have an automatic network for job searching—the teachers and administrators in the school where you are assigned. Many student teachers want to get jobs where they student teach because of proximity to their college campus and friends, and because they feel that they have inside knowledge of that school and wouldn't have quite so many shocks the first year. If you want a job where you student teach, then you must make an exceptionally good impression during that semester. Just as you feel you know the school, the school administrators and teachers will feel that they know you, and that can help or hinder getting the job there! It's a similar situation to being a substitute teacher as a means of getting your foot in the door.

In addition to networking right in the school where you teach, consider attending a state or national conference to talk with other teachers about where the jobs are. You can also e-mail recent graduates in their first year of teaching to inquire about openings in the districts that hired them.

Remember to be professional about networking. It is not professional to call a friend whose relative is on a school board and ask for special favors. If you do hear of an opening from an acquaintance, verify the opening by going to a website and getting official information about the position. Do not start a cover letter by saying that your aunt Tillie's cousin said she heard of a 3rd-grade position becoming available at Lincoln Elementary School because Ms. Teachforever finally retired at 68. While networking can be a powerful tool, don't let it be your only source of information.

Your college professors are a good source to talk with about job openings. They are often out in the schools visiting student teachers and many times know of openings that may arise. Many times professors receive calls from principals late in the summer for high-needs teaching fields and for last-minute openings due to increased enrollment. While professors and directors of career centers are not supposed to say, "Well, the best candidate we have is Kerry Baker," they can let you know of a last-minute opening and you can say that you were referred by the professor or career center director. Some career centers get your permission to send out contact information on candidates based on your field of teaching, if such a call is received in the office. Then, the office can release the name and e-mail or phone number of all the newly certified teachers in a field who are still job searching. Many people like face-to-face networking at a job fair as a preferred way to job search.

THE ROLE OF JOB FAIRS IN YOUR SEARCH

The Purposes of Job Fairs

Just as there are a variety of websites to help you find a job, there are a variety of purposes of job fairs. Some job fairs are informational. These fairs will provide information about districts' predicted need for new hires, what the district is like to live in, and other pertinent information. At other fairs, recruiters are gathering résumés to take back to the district to be sorted and evaluated by the personnel office and perhaps building principals. At some job fairs, personnel directors and building-level administrators give short interviews and then use those interviews to decide who will receive on-site interviews. In a few cases, interviewers arrive at job fairs with contracts in hand to offer the strongest students.

Teacher job fairs are held at most colleges and universities in the early spring, and sometimes in the fall, depending on the number of teachers who graduate and the job market. In order to participate, watch for registration through the career center. Some colleges will also hold a job fair off-campus, but near the jobs. For example, if your university is in a small town but there are many job openings in a big city, the college may hold the job fair in the city for the convenience of the recruiters.

Districts also hold job fairs, either individually or as a consortium. When a district holds its own fair, it is certainly in need of new teachers. Most district-level job fairs are advertised by your college career center and on the district and state websites. Watch for these fairs by reading the websites, register in advance if required, then make your preparations to go. See chapter 4 in this book for how to prepare for the job fair.

To review, if you want a teaching job, you have to find a job opening at a school. How do you do that? Use your college career center as a starting place for local job postings and for information about campus fairs. Use a variety of online websites for searching, including district, state, and national commercial ones. Go to job fairs at your campus and in various school districts to find jobs that are available. Last, do not depend on rumors for a teaching job, but do network with others in education.

A WORD ABOUT WANT ADS

If you live in a large city and seek a job in that large city, then newspaper want ads can be a good source for job openings. If you don't subscribe, try the local or campus library issues of the *New York Times*, *Atlanta Journal Constitution*, *Chicago Tribune*, *Los Angeles Times*, *Washington Post*, or other big city papers. The back pages of *Education Week* also carry ads for teachers. *Education Week* can probably be found in your college library or the dean's office, as it is a periodical for academics and school administrators. Small towns rarely use want ads in local papers to advertise teaching jobs, but if your interest is in a large city, the want ads may be of use.

Once a job opening is found, no matter how it is found, it is time for your paperwork to speak for you. You need a professional cover letter, résumé, and

portfolio that set you apart from the crowd if you want to find the right teach- .
ing job for you.

JOB SEARCH CHECKLIST

1. Get to know the college career center personnel and the services offered by them at least a year before you want a job.
2. Read the college career center job postings regularly.
3. Make a credentials file with the career center that includes three to five
   letters of recommendation.
4. Find state websites that meet your needs and read them regularly.
5. Read one or more books on the teacher education job search.
6. Talk/network with other recent graduates who are new teachers, as
   well as other teachers and administrators.
7. Consider out-of-state teaching because it may be where the jobs are.
8. Gather a "career wardrobe"—have at least one suit that is appropriate
   for the job fair.
9. Attend several job fairs at colleges and in districts.
10. Start your search no later than January for positions in August.

TO CONSIDER

1. Spend some time searching online for sites that are most helpful to you.
   Find at least three that you will go back to on a daily or weekly basis to
   use.
2. Look in your closet and pick the best outfit for attending a job fair. If
   nothing seems appropriate, buy something new, or enlist the help of
   family or friends to get together and give you career clothes for the next
   upcoming holiday or birthday.
3. Write down the contacts you might already have for discussing job
   openings in nearby districts. Who else should you cultivate as a contact?

3

The Paperwork

In chapter 4 of this book, you will learn about behavior-based interviewing, BBI, a style of interviewing that has long been used in the business world and is growing in use in teacher interviews. The premise behind behavior-based interviewing is that past behavior is the best predictor of future behavior. The behavior-based approach to evaluating paperwork can also be used. Future employers will look at your cover letter, résumé, and portfolio and make a judgment about your future performance based on the paperwork. Well-organized, skillfully written paperwork is an indicator that you are organized and skillful. A few typos or misspelled words indicate that your work is sloppy, and principals do not like to field complaints from parents about misspelled words in letters sent home. With this in mind, what should your cover letter reveal about you?

THE COVER LETTER

The cover letter is your introduction to the potential employer. It always accompanies a résumé that is sent in response to finding an opening. It is an advertisement that sells you in a succinct and businesslike manner. It should be an example of your best possible writing—in both content and form. The cover letter should only be one page in length. It must contain the following pertinent information:

1. Your current address
2. The date written

3. The name of the potential employer and address
4. The job opening for which you are applying
5. (Optional) How you found out about the opening
6. Statement of your full or anticipated certification and graduation
7. One or two relevant facts about your previous teaching experience (student teaching experience counts)
8. One thing that makes you stand out from 42 or 102 other applicants
9. Information on how you can be contacted

No small or unusual fonts should be used. Twelve-point is a minimum font size, and letters should generally be double spaced or space and a half. Don't try to cram too much information in with a smaller font, single spacing, or extended margins. Employers often wear bifocals and need to see clear letters!

Stop now and write out the following details. Write about what makes your background special. Did you complete a yearlong student teaching placement or have field experiences in more than two schools? Did you work in a high-needs or high-priority district with students of diversity? Do you speak a foreign language? Have you tutored students in after-school programs? Did you direct a summer camp or vacation Bible school?

Each time that you find a job vacancy posted, read it and write down the specifics of the job description. Compare the needs listed in the description to your qualifications. If they match—apply! Make sure your cover letter highlights how they match, so that you get the employer's attention even before your résumé is reviewed.

Special Cover Letter Questions

1. *Do employers really care if my signature is legible?* The answer is yes, generally they do. If you can't sign your name legibly, how will your handwriting look on the board to students? When parents get a letter from their child's teacher, they want to be able to read the signature.
2. *Does it matter how I found the job opening?* Yes, it can matter. If you found the job opening on the district's website, that indicates that you have read their site and know some background on the district. Simply reporting that you found the job opening on a state or national website is an indication of your technology skills. If your cooperating teacher from student teaching teaches at the school or district and told you of the opening, you may certainly write that. It will inform a personnel director immediately that you have some experience in the district. However, if your aunt's second cousin told you about the job, don't write that. Research the opening a little further and indicate that you read of the opening, after you really do read of it.

3. *If I am an art teacher, or a creative 2nd-grade teacher, can I make my cover letter unique, perhaps on construction paper, or as a colorful brochure?* No, the cover letter should be businesslike. Save your creativity for some examples in your portfolio.

4. *Does it matter to whom I address the cover letter? Should it just be to "Dear Sir/Madam"?* The cover letter must be addressed to the person listed in the job posting. Write their name and title as it appears in the job posting. If no name is given, then you address the letter to the title/entity listed in the job posting, with the address given, and then start your letter. Do not use "To whom it may concern."

Your return address and phone

Name of individual personnel director/principal
District address

Mr./Ms. Last name:

First paragraph:

- State position for which you are applying and where you found the position.
- State your certification and/or anticipated graduation date.

Second paragraph:

- Sell yourself!
- One or two highlights of your education/career/experience.
- A reference to your enclosed résumé.

Third paragraph

- State that you have submitted your letters of recommendation/credentials file.
- Request the district's application or state when you submitted it.
- A positive ending line, "I look forward to an opportunity to meet with you and interview for the position at _____ school."

Sincerely,
SIGN YOUR NAME LEGIBLY IN BLACK INK

Keep this letter to ONLY one page.

Figure 3.1.   Worksheet for One Great Cover Letter

114 Carter Hall, State University
Collegetown, State 12343
February 21, 200_

Ms. Sarah Smith, Director of Personnel
Lincoln School District
300 School Road
Town, State 12366

Ms. Smith:

I am writing this letter to apply for the job opening posted on the state website for a 5th-grade teacher at Garden Lakes Elementary School. As my enclosed résumé indicates, I will graduate in May and receive full certification for elementary education at that time, as I have already passed the state certification test.

I am currently completing my student teaching at College Park Elementary School, only 25 miles from your district, in a combined 4th- and 5th-grade placement. In addition to my student teaching, I have volunteered to work two afternoons a week in the school's after-school enrichment program. I have learned how much supplemental activities can help students who would otherwise have no supervision during this time. I am very interested in the position at Garden Lakes because it matches my student teaching experience, and because of the school's innovative before- and after-school programs.

I have completed your district's online application, and my credentials file and transcripts have been requested and should arrive at your office within 10 days. I can be contacted by phone at 123-234-5678 or by e-mail at student@stateu.edu. I look forward to the opportunity to interview for the position at Garden Lakes.

Sincerely,

Sarah Student

Figure 3.2.   Sample Cover Letter for New Graduate

123 Maple Street
Anytown, State 98765
March 1, 200_

Mr. Clark Kerry, Assistant Superintendent
Consolidated School System
`22 School Street
Town, State 98123

Mr. Kerry:

Please accept this letter and my résumé as an applicant for the high
school mathematics position advertised on your district's website. As a
fully certified secondary teacher with four years of teaching experience, I
feel that my experience teaching 10th- and 11th-grade math courses at
Roosevelt High has prepared me well for the position described at
Cartersville High School. The highlight of my teaching career to date was
being a part of a curriculum mapping team that worked to help raise our
school's SAT math scores significantly.

As my enclosed résumé outlines, I have coached the Engineering Team,
as well as organized multiple school dances while working at Roosevelt.
I have enjoyed the students and faculty at Roosevelt, but my family needs
to live closer to the city, and therefore the Cartersville position meets my
professional needs.

I would like to request that your school's application be sent to me at the
above address. Upon receipt of the application, I will ensure that my letters of recommendation and transcripts are sent to your office. Thank you
in advance for your consideration and I would appreciate the opportunity
to interview in your district. I can be reached at work from 1:00 to 1:50
p.m. at 123-900-8788 or at home at 799-000-5677. My e-mail is
teacher@aol.com.

Sincerely,

Lynn Teacher

Figure 3.3.   Sample Cover Letter for an Experienced Teacher

THE RÉSUMÉ

The résumé is you—at a glance—and a glance is all that some administrators will give to each résumé. Therefore, the résumé is of top importance. Your résumé is sent to a district with your cover letter whenever you apply for a job opening. Do not send a résumé without a cover letter. If you are hired, the résumé is one of the first pieces of paperwork that goes into your personnel file. If you are not hired, or even if not interviewed, your résumé may be kept for a short amount of time in the files of a personnel director, just in case they need to contact more people for interviews. Some districts get hundreds of résumés for each position that is open, and do not keep them, even for a limited time. Copies of your résumé should be taken with you to the job fair.

Here are some basic rules for résumés:

1. Never embellish or misrepresent information about yourself. (In other words, don't lie!) Misrepresentation of information will always catch up with you and you will lose your job. In some states, you may lose your teacher certification/license as well. Besides, it's just wrong!
2. Never send a résumé out that hasn't been proofread by at least two other people. Use your friends, professors, other teachers, or the professionals at the career center to read and give you feedback on your résumé.
3. You should not include personal information such as marital status, health, physical condition, or religious preferences.
4. Don't leave holes in your education or work experience. If you completed military duty, dropped out of college to travel, or left teaching for a few years to work in business, include lines about that work. Having gaps in work experience isn't a problem unless you can't explain the gaps.
5. All words must be spelled correctly. Use an easy-to-read font, and leave space so that the résumé is easy to read. You may use bullets and phrases—you do not have to have all complete sentences.
6. Use good paper, white or buff-colored, to match your cover letter.
7. You should read other good examples of résumés before writing yours. See the career center for examples, or use one of the many books published that contain sample résumés. See examples later in this chapter.

Special Questions About Teacher Résumés

1. *What do I do about accounting for time out from teaching to start my family? Doesn't this reveal too much about my personal life?* The answer to this question is, "It all depends." Being a parent can be good background experience for being a teacher. You can put a line on your résumé

about being a volunteer, if that was included in the time you spent being a stay-at-home parent. Some people choose to write "Stay-at-home parent: volunteered at local parents' morning out, raised funds for kindergarten library, and attended meetings for assertive parenting." Employers know that over 75 percent of teachers are females and that many have chosen teaching because it is a family-friendly profession. If you learned new things while staying at home and starting your family, you may choose to sell that in your résumé. Parenting skills are important ones.

2. *How long should teacher résumés be?* A new teacher who is a recent graduate, who has student taught but never been employed full time before, should have a one-page résumé. A teacher with a few years of full-time teaching experience may have a one- to two-page résumé. Even someone with years of experience in the business world should limit his or her résumé to one to two pages. Why? Busy employers don't have time to read more.

3. *What does the employer really want to know?* They want to know if you are fully certified and have had experience at the grade or subject level for the job opening posted. They want to know where you earned your degree. They want to know if you have any special skills, such as coaching.

4. *Do I include high school awards?* No. Employers do not need to know about high school awards or experiences unless they relate directly to your job objective as a new teacher. If you want to coach a sport, and played that sport in high school, winning the MVP award would be noteworthy. If you were the editor of your high school yearbook, and want to be the yearbook sponsor, you may include it.

5. *Do I list my college awards?* Again, college awards should be limited on a résumé for a teaching job. List only those that may relate to your future teaching or are very prestigious. If you won a college work award for three years of dedicated work for the same position, list that, as it indicates your perseverance.

6. *What is the difference between a curriculum vitae and a résumé?* A curriculum vitae is a list of one's life work. Some college professors maintain a vita that is over ten pages long because they are required to document all of their professional papers and presentations. A teaching résumé does not do this. Sending a ten-page résumé to a potential employer will probably get you nowhere, since the employer will wonder why you are even looking for a teaching job. As you seek administrative positions in education, such as an assistant principal job, you may have a longer résumé (two to three pages).

7. *How do I shorten my résumé if I do have several years of experience doing other things?* For example, a candidate with a master's degree in sci-

ence worked several years in higher education as a research assistant, thinking she might pursue a doctorate and become a professor. Upon the birth of her second child, she earned teacher certification to pursue high school teaching. She wasn't getting responses to her eight-page résumé that listed all the grants and research work she had completed with professors. Why not? High school principals hire people who can *teach* five or six classes a day, not spend time researching and writing. Employers were afraid that she would be far too theoretical to teach high school classes. She was hired immediately when she used a one-page résumé that highlighted her master's degree in science and her newly earned teacher certification. She reduced six years of work in higher education into a few lines. The fact that all six years of work in higher education were in one school was also in her favor, as principals like to see candidates who stay at one job.

How Do I Start to Write My Résumé?

The best way to begin writing a résumé is to look at the following worksheet and start writing out your information about each section. Strategies for each section follow.

Identity

Yes, you need to be available in order for districts to contact you. Many new graduates list two addresses. The first is where they are now, on campus, and the second is where they will be after graduation. List a date for the permanent address—it's okay if it's your parents' home. After you graduate, update the address information. Cell phones and e-mail addresses should be included. Hints: Have a professional message on your voice mail—not one that makes you sound like a crazy college kid. If you list your e-mail address on a résumé, check it daily.

Job Objective or Certification

You are either certified or not. You may write a line that says, "Full certification awarded upon graduation, May 17, 2009." Some people write "Eligible for full certification upon graduation, May 17, 2009." If you have not yet passed a state certification test, then you *cannot* write "eligible for certification upon graduation." You must write "Eligible upon successful completion of the state test and graduation." Don't mince words here. Being certified is like being pregnant. You either are or you are not. Once you pass the state test and graduate, update your résumé!

Do not write a flowery job objective about teaching every child to self-actualize and learn to be true to his or her heart's desire. If you are looking for a job in your area of certification, you do not need to put a job objective on your résumé, since the certification/licensure says it all. You may put a job objective if you want to lessen or broaden your job prospects. For example:

Certification earned: Elementary education, K–6 state certificate, May, 2006.

Job objective: Seeking a classroom position in kindergarten or first grade.

This job objective limits the candidate's options, telling the employer that he or she only wants two grade levels.

Certification: Licensure for 7–12 social studies will be completed upon graduation, May 20, 2008. Coaching endorsement (football and soccer) completed.

Job objective: To obtain a high school teaching position in social studies and coach football and/or soccer.

This candidate has greatly enhanced his or her job prospects by listing the coaching endorsement and his or her objective to coach these sports. Remember that if you say you will do something, you must follow through. This candidate may want to list high school sports activities, as well as college ones.

Education

This is very important. List the colleges you have attended for degrees and significant work, beginning with the most recent. For example, if you are graduating from Anystate University, list it first, and list your major and minor. If you transferred to Anystate University from Lincoln Community College, where you earned an associate's degree, list that under the university that granted your bachelor's degree. If you have been a student at Anystate University for four years, and only went to another college for two summer courses to complete a requirement, you do not need to list that work. It will be on your transcript, anyway.

What if you earned a bachelor's degree from one college, then your teacher licensure elsewhere? The rule still holds about placing the most recent work first, especially since the employer wants to know where you learned to be a teacher. Examples:

B.S. Degree, West Georgia State University, May 2008
Major: Elementary Education, 3.7/4.0 GPA

A.A. Degree, Georgia Highlands Community College, May 2006
Major: Pre-education; completed all general studies

Or

Teacher Certification, Secondary English
State University, Springfield, NJ, May 2008

B.A. Degree, Trenton College, NJ, May 2000
Major: English; Minor: Business

It is generally acceptable to put your grade point average on a résumé when it helps your case! If you attended a small college that the employer does not immediately recognize, you should include the city and state. If your university has several branches, include the state, such as University of Illinois at Urbana-Champaign, or University of Illinois at Springfield.

Teaching and Work Experience

Your most recent teaching experiences go first. For new graduates, that means student teaching. Write the most important information that the employer wants to know, and sometimes this information changes based on the job for which you are applying. This is where word processing becomes the most wonderful tool in the world!
Examples:

Butterfield Elementary School, Lincoln, NE, Spring 2009
Student taught 29 fifth graders, all subjects
Lead teacher for three weeks; developed units in language arts and math

Tyler Elementary School, Shawnee, NE, Fall 2008
10-week field experience in 2nd and 3rd grades
Wrote and taught six lessons

Martin Luther King Primary, Lincoln, NE, Spring 2008
Completed 40 hours of observation in kindergarten and first grades
Tutored three children in math

Teachers with experience do not need to list field experiences from college, but may still want to include student teaching. Employers want to know about your full-time experience once you have started a career.
Example:

Youngstown Middle School, Youngstown, OH, August 2006–June 2008
Taught five classes daily of 7th-grade language arts

Supervised the state reading assessment tests for 6th, 7th, and 8th grades
Completed the at-risk reading endorsement

Washington Elementary School, Belleville, OH, Spring 2006
Student taught in 6th-, 7th-, and 8th-grade language arts
Lead teacher for two weeks; worked with 26 ELL students in classes

As these examples show, years of work can be summarized in two to three lines on a résumé. Remember to highlight your experience in the areas listed as needed in the job description.

Related Work Experience/Special Skills

The kinds of related work experience that will make your résumé stand out include work where you organized, directed, or taught in another setting, or provided orientation or training to children, teenagers, or adults. Working at summer camps, volunteering with Boy Scouts, Girl Scouts, or 4-H, or providing orientation for new hires at a summer job are all excellent examples. Employers are also looking for longevity in other jobs. A candidate who worked three years in food service in her dorm shows that she can persevere in a job—no matter how nonglamorous the position. That candidate may get a second look by the employer because she stayed with the position. A candidate who works for four Christmas breaks as a customer service representative at a department store will be seen as someone who can indeed handle parent complaints.

Examples:

Caterpillar Day Care, Ducktown, MS, Summers, 2006, 2007
Teacher's aide for 3- and 4-year-olds
Planned and taught afternoon mini-lessons
Provided parent orientation

Mississippi State University, Summers, 2004, 2005
Orientation guide for freshmen
Wrote and presented "What your young adult won't tell you about life in the dorms" for nine parent orientation weekends

The last category of related experience sometimes includes the areas of special skills and memberships and awards. Again, never embellish here, but if you do have a special skill, don't hesitate to wow the potential employer with it. What might be a special skill? Speaking a foreign language; having experience teaching swimming, crafts, gymnastics, music, or computers; or having traveled extensively are all skills that make teachers more interesting people. The awards you list should only be ones that are from college, and once you are an experienced teacher, you probably won't include those.

References

You have a couple of options here. If your college provides a credentials file service, use it, and then just write "Credentials on file" and the address, phone, and e-mail of the career center that provides that service. If not, you may want to write a line such as "References available upon request." Very few new teachers list their references with contact information on the résumé. After all, your résumé is only *one page* in length if you are a new teacher, and only one to two pages if you are an experienced veteran at teaching.

Identity: address, phone number, and e-mail where you can be reached by employers

Job objective or certification(s):

    To obtain a teaching position in grades _____. Or
    Certification: Certified for the teaching of _____ in grades _____ in
    (name of state).

Education:
List the dates for each college or university attended, including degrees earned, and major and minor areas of study. Begin with the most recent.

Teaching and work experience:
List the dates for your teaching, student teaching, and field experiences in education, along with location. Include other pertinent work experiences (summer jobs, camps, full- or part-time employment before teaching). List by most recent first.

Related experience/special skills:
Highlight special training (computers, languages), volunteer work, or awards. List by date, beginning with the most recent.

References:
Ask your cooperating teacher, college supervisor, and a college professor to serve as references. Include their addresses, phone numbers, and e-mail addresses. Former principals and supervisors from other jobs may be used.

Figure 3.4.   You at a Glance—The Résumé Worksheet

Sara N. Tayler

Present Address	Address after May 12, 2009:
112 College Street	111 Maple Drive
University City, State 98765	Hometown, State 87654
(233) 123-0987	(233) 234-0987
e-mail: stayler@student.edu	e-mail: taylerfam@aol.com

Certification:
Elementary Education, K–6, upon graduation, May 2009
Passed state tests, March 2009

Education:
B.S., State University, City, State, May 2009
Major: Elementary Education, 3.33/4 GPA
Included a summer abroad in England, 2008

Teaching Experience:
Camp Creek Primary School, Camp Creek, GA
Yearlong student teaching, 2008–2009
One semester, 4th grade, one semester, 3rd grade
Lead teaching for four weeks; included work with early intervention/priority students
Developed and taught three interdisciplinary units
Tutored remedial students for state reading tests

College Lab School, University City, Spring 2008
Observed 50 hours in kindergarten, 1st, and 2nd grades
Taught a weeklong reading unit; taught six math lessons

Related Experiences/Awards:
Western 4-H Camp, Jacksonville, AL: Served as cabin counselor, Summer 2005; Directed arts and crafts, Summer 2006; Assistant camp director and cabin counselor trainer, Summer 2007
Instructor of aerobics, Waters Dorm, State University, 2005–2007
Recipient of the Waters Dorm Outstanding Volunteer Award, 2007

Credentials Available:
Career Center
136 College Street, Box 201
University City, State, 98765
(120) 445-5567 or e-mail: career@stateu.edu

Figure 3.5. Sample Résumé for New Graduate

Tate M. Carl
114 Maple Grove Drive
Anytown, State 65432
Phone: 607-770-1973 or Cell: 607-908-1234
e-mail: tatemc@mail.net

Job Objective:
To teach middle grades math and science, and to coach soccer and/or basketball

Education:
Teacher Certification, State University, Carrollton, December, 2010
Certification earned in middle grades math and science

B.S. Degree, Any State University, Carrollton, May 2007
Major: Math

A.A. Degree, Columbus Community College, Columbus, Maryland
May 2004
Major: General studies

Teaching Experience:
Columbus Middle School, Fall 2010
Taught up to six classes daily; lead teacher for two weeks
Implemented a homework hotline for 7th-grade team
Assisted with 8th-grade basketball
Chaperoned 8th-grade planetarium trip

Completed 100 hours of practicum observations in three Jackson County middle schools; taught 15 lessons; tutored 35 hours

Other Work Experience:
Amco Insurance Company, May 2004–June 2008
Included part-time and full-time work
Worked as statistician, claims specialist, and researcher
Provided orientation for specialists on quarterly reports
Interpreted sales figures at two annual meetings
Supervised development of departmental website

Awards and Memberships:
Kappa Delta Pi Honor Society member, 2006–present
Recipient of local Kappa Delta Pi student teaching award
Amco Insurance Appreciation Award, 2006
Columbus Soccer League coach of the summer, 2006

References available upon request.
My teaching portfolio is available for view at www.myport.tate

Figure 3.6.   Sample Résumé for Experienced Teacher

LETTERS OF RECOMMENDATION

The college career center is again the first place to look for help with letters of recommendation, since the center may provide you with the services of a credentials file. A credentials file contains three to five letters of recommendation and can be mailed to the districts by the career center for you. The service may be free, or there may be a charge. Additionally, the letters can be mailed electronically. The big advantage of using a credentials file service is that the people who write your letters only write the letter once, and then you can send the letters to an infinite number of school districts.

If no credentials file service exists, then you must get writers to send letters to the districts where you apply. Always read the district application carefully to see if individuals need to write letters, or if there are forms to be completed. Many districts now require you to give three recommendation forms to writers, and then the writers complete the forms, adding letters if required. In districts with their own forms and requirements, a credentials package of letters must be supplemented with the correct forms, completed by those who know your work. The rule is always this: do what the district says to do with regard to the application process. Failure to follow the district guidelines will mean that you don't get the interview. Unlike your parents, and some of your professors, the school district's personnel director will not remind you of what to do. Another hint: Do the paperwork on time and make sure it is sent to the correct office.

Who should write your letters of recommendation? Your cooperating teacher for student teaching is the first person who should write a letter on your behalf. He or she has seen you teach more than anyone else. If you are a new graduate and you do not get a letter from your cooperating teacher, that is a "red flag" to some employers. Red flags are warnings that something may not be quite right. Perhaps you couldn't get along with your assigned teacher for a semester? Perhaps he or she disapproved of your methods or skills? Try to get a positive letter from this teacher. The only thing worse than no letter from your cooperating teacher is a negative letter. If you feel that the letter would be a negative one, then ask others who have seen you teach for their letters.

After you have been a full-time teacher and are changing jobs, then the letter of recommendation from your current principal or assistant principal becomes the critical one. Anytime you start a new job search, you need new letters of recommendation. Update your credentials file for each search, even if there is a fee to do so as an alum of the college or university.

Hint: Credentials files may be open or closed. Find out when establishing your file which is the case at your university. If you can choose open or closed, consider the options. With an open file, you may go to the career center and read the letters on file. If one is negative, you may remove it. With a closed file, you may not review or remove a letter from your file. Why do some students choose closed files and why might some employers want such a file? Some employers may feel that letters in a closed file are the most honest about a candidate's skills.

Your college supervisor is another important person who should provide you with a letter of recommendation. In areas where the university and the school districts work closely together, employers know the professors well and consider their letters to be of great value. A professor on campus who knows your work can also write a letter for you. If you are a middle or high school candidate, a letter from a major professor that attests to your knowledge of subject content can be crucial to have in your file.

Who else can write letters on your behalf? A former employer, even if not in teaching, can provide excellent insight into your work habits, and positive past behavior is the best predictor of future performance. Your part-time job supervisor, or a supervisor from a summer job can provide a good letter.

The Best Hints for Getting Letters of Recommendation

1. Allow the writers plenty of time. Teachers, professors, and job supervisors are very busy people. Allow them a minimum of two to three weeks to get your letter to the campus career center or the school district. Asking late and needing a letter immediately does not speak well of your organizational skills.
2. Provide writers with addressed, stamped envelopes. This indicates your thoughtfulness for the writers' time and work. Sending multiple letters for 20 or 30 students a year can be expensive!
3. Provide writers with the appropriate forms.
4. If a professor has worked with you, but not during your senior year, give them a copy of your teaching résumé, so that they are aware of what you did in student teaching.
5. Thank the writer profusely. A little bit of chocolate goes a long way and is appreciated!

A TEACHER'S PORTFOLIO

Portfolios and portfolio assessment have been buzzwords in education for years now. Many student teachers must complete a portfolio in order to graduate from their program. These program assessment portfolios are often in three- or four-inch binders that contain mountains of artifacts with cover sheets. An interview portfolio is *not* such a portfolio. The interview portfolio is sleek, organized, and is used as a visual aid when you are interviewed. While developing your résumé and cover letter, build your portfolio so that you will be ready when an employer invites you to interview.

Your portfolio should fit neatly into a small three-ring binder (not more than one and one-half inches on the spine). Leather binders with zippers look exceptionally professional. Placing documents in plastic sheet protectors in the binder will protect them. You may want to place an extra copy of your résumé and a photocopy of your teacher certification at the beginning of the portfolio. There should be no more than 10 other documents in the portfolio. These may include:

1. A lesson plan that you have used and that was successful
2. A sample letter to parents about the beginning of the school year or a new semester
3. A list of rules, consequences, and positives that you have used in a classroom
4. A sample unit plan (one to three pages) or curriculum map that you used
5. One or two samples of student work, with the student's name removed (You can use these to explain how your teaching impacted student learning.)
6. One or two pictures of a bulletin board or learning center that you created in your past work, to explain how you set up a classroom or to explain special projects
7. A picture of former students engaged in an activity you organized

Use of the Portfolio

Once you have created this beautiful document, how will you use it? First of all, do not expect a busy interviewer to say, "Please show me your portfolio and explain what is in it." This is not going to happen. If it does, limit what you say to explaining the most pertinent artifacts—your lesson plan, your parent letters, and your management plan.

The best use of a portfolio is as a visual aid. When an interviewer says "Tell me how you have planned lessons," you open your portfolio and respond, "Here is a sample lesson plan that worked beautifully." You will continue to explain how all of your plans include student objectives, a variety of learning experiences, and an assessment. The same is true when the interviewer asks you how you have handled classroom management in the past. You open the portfolio to your classroom management plan and say, "This is the plan I used in student teaching. It worked well with 5th graders because they needed rules, positives, and corrective actions." More on using the portfolio will be addressed in the interview chapter.

Online Portfolios

What does an electronic portfolio look like?

1. A website or web page you maintain that includes the same samples listed earlier for the paper portfolio (sample lesson plans, management rules and consequences, and so forth)
2. A set of documents on a compact disc that can be sent to an employer or taken to the interview

The downside of electronic portfolios is that the employer simply may not have the time to review your website or disc. If you take a disc with you, chances are it may not be compatible with equipment in the office where you interview, and the employer will not have time for you to "install" or demonstrate your portfolio in this manner. There is certainly no time for viewing at a job fair.

Why have an electronic portfolio at all? A few employers may read on your résumé that you have an electronic portfolio and go to your site to view it. I recently viewed a student teacher's electronic portfolio that included a six-minute video clip of his teaching. The clip showed him teaching physical exercise to 2nd graders and it was indeed impressive. Had I been an administrator, that clip would have earned him an interview with me. Just having the electronic portfolio indicates that you're technology savvy. A few candidates are leaving CDs with interviewers at job fairs. I don't recommend including one with your résumé and cover letter, however. In the future, everyone may be using more technology, but for now, paperwork remains the primary source of information for the employer.

When your cover letters and résumés arrive at school districts, you can expect some calls for screening interviews or on-site interviews. With your portfolio polished and ready, as well as your career clothes, it's time to talk about interviewing.

4

The Interviews

ALL ABOUT BEHAVIOR-BASED INTERVIEWING

BBI Comes From the Business World

Behavior-based interviewing (BBI) comes from the business world, where it has been used successfully for at least two decades. Time is money in business, and when hiring, employers need to know if the candidate has the background and experience to do the job. There is such a need for highly qualified teachers, that time is invaluable in education, too. School administrators need to know if the future teacher has the background and experience to do the job, and to do it well.

The premise of behavior-based interviewing is that past behavior is the best predictor of future performance. BBI questions are not simply "Tell me about yourself," "What might you do if . . . ?" or "Where do you see yourself in five years?" Rather, BBI questions require that the candidate talk about his or her previous experience with the topic of the question. BBI questions typically start with "Tell me about a time when . . . " "Describe an incident where . . ." or "How have you handled this issue in the past?"

The behavior-based interviewing style uses specific questions based on the skills, background, and experience that candidates should have in order to succeed at the tremendously challenging and unique job of teaching. So, you may be asking, "What are the skills and experiences that one needs to be a successful teacher, and how do I get these skills in order to get my first job?" It's an age-old problem: "How do I get a job to get experience, and how do I get experience to get a job?" Chapter 1 discussed teacher certification and the skills you need to know in order to teach as you learn those skills in teacher education course work. Student teaching is the number one way that prospective teachers get experience with the issues, challenges, and day-to-day demands of teaching.

Let's review what teachers need to know:

1. The subject matter that they teach (content)
2. How students learn (child development/educational psychology)
3. How to motivate students to want to learn
4. Curriculum (what to teach/how to meet state standards in the content area)
5. Methods (how to teach the specific subjects)
6. How to manage and discipline a class
7. How to assess, evaluate, and grade student work
8. How to meet the needs of diverse students, including special education students, gifted students, and language minority students
9. How to communicate with colleagues and administrators (being a team player)
10. How to communicate with parents and how to be a public relations expert with parents and the community
11. How to stay current in your subject-matter field and the field of teaching (professionalism)

Questions Based on What Teachers Need to Know

You will be hired as a teacher only if you can show that you have the knowledge and experience in the skill areas listed above. Employers ask questions in each of the areas, and your answers must showcase your previous work in each area. After all, you are proving that you have the past behavior needed for a successful future performance.

Let's look at one performance area and see what might be asked. Since "what we teach" is so important, and so tied to state standards and high-stakes testing, teachers must know about curriculum and standards. A typical question in this area is, "Describe a lesson that you have taught that included a state-mandated curriculum standard." Early in teacher education courses, candidates learn what the state-mandated standards are and how to incorporate them into lessons. (Go to www.statestandards.com for links to individual states and their curriculum standards.) This question is a no-brainer for a graduate who taught a lot of lessons during field experiences and student teaching. It is a very tough question for a candidate who wasn't prepared in a good curriculum class, or who didn't student teach. This question alone separates candidates very quickly. BBI-style questions get at the heart of what a candidate must know and the candidate's answers are indicators of whether or not he or she can do the job.

What would be a good answer to the question, "Describe a lesson that you have taught that included a state-mandated curriculum standard"? A strong candidate might say,

> A lot of the state standards in language arts are aimed at getting students to be good writers. In my 5th-grade student teaching experience, I had the opportunity to implement a writers' workshop that not only met the state guidelines for getting students to write, but got the students to enjoy writing. They published little books and presented them by sitting in the author's chair. Those lessons with the writers' workshop taught me that we can meet the standards creatively, and get children to learn at a higher level. Of course, I made sure that when they wrote, they learned grammar and spelling, which will be on the state test for 5th graders.

Obviously, this answer indicates knowledge, experience, and enthusiasm for teaching. This answer will get you a job.

Knowing About vs. Doing the Skill

It can be argued that some candidates may be able to talk about a teaching skill without being able to stand in front of 28 seventh graders and actually "perform" the skill. However, the opposite argument makes even more sense. A candidate who cannot even talk about a skill will certainly not know how to implement it. The following two answers to questions about grading serve as examples.

A very commonly asked interview question for teachers is, "Describe how you set up a grading scale for students in your class." A strong candidate quickly outlines a clear system, perhaps based on total points, that can be used on a computer program or can be averaged easily with a calculator. The candidate gets a high evaluation for the answer when he or she adds, "Grades should never be secret. My students will be 9th graders and they should be able to keep track of their points and know their grade on any given day during the nine weeks. As a teacher, I will explain this system at the beginning of the year, and at the beginning of each new grading period."

A candidate who says, "Grading can be so tough, and students always want to argue about it," will not get a high score for this answer. A candidate who can't answer this question with some degree of authority probably doesn't know where to begin to set up a grading scale, and will encounter problems when a student asks, "How are we being graded?"

Teachers will always be asked about classroom management and discipline issues. When asked, "Tell me about the kinds of rules you have used in managing your class," you need to give a short overview of three to five rules that have worked well. Good rules are observable and enforceable and in effect all the time. State the rules simply: "Keep hands, feet, and objects to yourself," or "Be in your seat when the bell rings." A really strong candidate will indicate the book or author that was read as background to building a management plan, and then outline how these rules were especially helpful during student teaching. (See the bibliography of this book for good recommendations of what to read about management.)

A candidate who answers the management question with "I am not going to start out with rules, rewards, or consequences, because I want the students to like me," won't get hired. The principal's life is too short to watch this candidate go down in flames by October when the students are walking all over him or her and the new teacher is screaming at students, wondering why they don't behave.

An important point to remember is that you are "teaching" the interviewer the way you would "teach" a class. When asked how you set up a grading scale or how you created your management plan, begin by saying, "Here's exactly what I tell my students. . . ." A good interviewer knows that if you can teach him or her about the topic, then you can teach your students. Good interviewing is an opportunity to spotlight your good teaching!

The interviewer needs to know that you have good communication skills for working with parents. How you answer questions in an interview indicates how you will answer parent questions. Parents will ask, "How is my child's work being graded in your class?" and "What are the rules for my child's behavior in your class?" Have answers ready for the interview and ready for the parents by the first open house.

BBI Interview Formats and Evaluation

Interviewers who are skilled in BBI will have a copy of the questions in front of them while they interview you. They will ask the same set of questions of each candidate who is a finalist for the position. The interviewers will take notes and evaluate your answers. Some interviewers rate each answer as you give it. Interviewers use numeric scales, such as:

$$1 \quad 2 \quad 3 \quad 4 \quad 5$$

1 indicates a very weak answer or no answer
2 indicates a below-average answer
3 indicates an average answer
4 indicates a fairly strong answer
5 indicates a very strong answer

Another way that interviewers evaluate answers is with a rubric for unacceptable, acceptable, and target answers. Here's what that means:

Unacceptable answers:

- include no answer provided
- are incorrect
- do not demonstrate "best practice" in teaching
- show that candidate has no past experience with situation
- show that candidate's past experience was not positive

Acceptable answers:

- meet the minimal standard
- show some past positive experience with situation
- are fairly articulate
- give indication that candidate will be able to perform the action in the future

Target answers:

- wow the interviewer
- include articulate, precise vocabulary
- go above and beyond what might be expected
- indicate past positive experience and knowledge of what was learned from the experience

Interviewers use BBI-style questions during on-site interviews, as well as for telephone interviews and job fair interviews. Knowing the basics of how these questions are worded, and knowing how you will be evaluated, will help you succeed at the preliminary interviews and the final interview.

To review BBI:

1. Behavior-based interviewing is grounded in the idea that past behavior is the best predictor of future performance.
2. In a job interview to be a teacher, you will be asked specific questions about the performance skills of teaching—curriculum, methods, management, grading, and so forth.
3. Strong candidates use their knowledge and experience to showcase their ability to do the many jobs of teaching.
4. One of the best hints for answering questions is to remember that interviewing is teaching. If you can teach the interviewer how you do something, you can teach the students.

HOW TO ANSWER BBI QUESTIONS USING PAR AND STAR

Whether you are answering questions in a telephone, job fair, or on-site interview, the acronyms of PAR and STAR will help you to organize your answers in a clear manner. PAR stands for problem, action, and result. Since many questions posed to candidates are about problems, you need to explain the problem that you have experienced, as it relates to the interviewer's question. It is not enough to describe past problems; you must then explain an action you took to resolve the problem, and the results of your action. For example, you may be asked to describe what you have done when students finish work at different rates. A PAR answer will sound like this:

> Working with 6th graders in my student teaching placement, there was much academic diversity. In fact, some of our 6th graders read at 2nd- and 3rd-grade levels, so I know what you mean about students finishing work at very different rates. (Problem) My teacher and I gave different assignments to different students, sometimes just cutting a worksheet in half, or providing the slower learners with the meanings of words, while others had to find the meanings themselves. Of course, we supplemented the work for advanced students, since we didn't want them to not learn as much because of the other students. (Action) It wasn't until I taught this class that I really learned the meaning of differentiated instruction. I also learned that reading really is the fundamental key to raising student achievement. (Result)

This kind of answer gets you a job! Here is what not to say:

> It would be so easy to teach students if they came to class on grade level. The hard part is knowing that you have to kind of "shoot to the middle" and hope that the weaker ones learn more this year. I've worked with remedial students and gifted, so I know I can do both. I think I heard once that teachers spend too much time reteaching. Maybe I would try tutors for the slower kids. Reteaching bores everybody. Maybe I would try games, too.

PAR keeps your answers organized. You should always be thinking about describing your experience with the problem in a positive way, then the action you took, or the action that you observed in a practicum. The result that you describe should also include what you learned, or as your college professors called it, your reflection on learning. Let's look at another example:

> Interview question: Describe a common student misbehavior for this grade level, and what you have done to correct the behavior.
> Candidate answer: I have learned that today's students talk out and blurt out whatever comes into their minds while in class. I saw this with little ones when

I had a practicum in 1st grade, and with the upper elementary students. (Problem) I now use a lot of think, pair, share activities and some think and write-a-word activities to combat this. I ask a question, then remind students to think 30 seconds, pair with the person next to them, and then share their answers. When a minute is up, then I ask for volunteers to raise their hands with possible answers. (Action) Not only did this help to resolve the problem, but the quality of the answers was 100 percent better. (Result)

What not to say:

I think that the noise level in my classroom in student teaching indicated the biggest student misbehavior—too much talking out of turn. I tried names on the board for talking, minutes after class, and nothing seemed to work. At one point I even flashed the lights to quiet the room. If the students were mine from the very beginning of the year, unlike in student teaching, I would be tougher from the start and they would be quiet. On the other hand, society seems to be noisier, so maybe classrooms are just going to be noisier.

Using STAR to Answer Questions

Not every question you will be asked in an interview should be about the problems and challenges of teaching. If a question is not directly about a problem, consider the STAR approach in answering. STAR represents situation, task, action, and result. As a teacher, you need to be able to sort out what is significant and what is not significant to a given teaching situation. You should be able to *briefly* describe situations, then talk about the task to be done, the action of implementing the task, and the results. For example, one of the teacher's many tasks is to motivate students. A future employer needs to know if you have motivated students in the past in order to know if you can motivate them after you are hired. To ascertain this, the employer may say, "Tell me about a time when you have motivated students to learn a challenging topic." A STAR answer follows:

The whole semester in geometry is considered dull and boring to some 10th-grade students. They look at the book and ask, "When will we ever really need this?" (Situation) The challenge is to make even geometry real and usable to them. (Task) This year, I started the geometry semester with a field trip out to the flagpole. I said that the principal had charged our class with replacing the ropes on the pole. If we could accurately measure how much rope was needed, and our findings netted a savings to the school over the outside consultant's replacement cost, then the amount saved would be used to reduce the cost of basketball tickets for our class. The students said, "For real?" "Yes," I replied, "this is the real deal." (Action) Well, suddenly they asked the right questions about finding the height of the pole, and we were ready to learn geometry. It worked well, and the principal followed through with discounted tickets for every member of that class. It was a fantastic activity that motivated and bonded the class. (Result)

What not to say:

> U.S. history is a required subject and by the time juniors in high school get around to the class, they feel that they know everything. They don't want to read, they don't want to discuss, and they seem to think that I'm the bad guy for making them do any work. U.S. history is important, so I tell them that they are adults and can make a choice: do the work or flunk. It really should be up to them at that point anyway.

The STAR approach is basically the same as PAR, only stated with different words. The important thing to remember is to keep your answer focused on what you have accomplished, seen, or experienced, and to communicate actions and results clearly. As an exercise, go back and read the answer about geometry and the flagpole aloud slowly, as if you were talking to someone. Time how long it takes to read that answer. It should take you about a minute. Before your first interview of any kind, practice some answers to the questions listed in this book. Look in the mirror while practicing and time your answers. Noted author and career specialist Robin Ryan says that 60-second answers are the best. In her book, *60 Seconds and You're Hired*, she encourages job seekers to practice answering questions in 60 seconds, because that's about how long interviewers will listen. Remember that past behavior is the best predictor of future performance, and if you bore the interviewer with too many insignificant details, he or she will perceive you to be someone who will bore your future classes in the same manner.

One final comment about PAR and STAR. PAR and STAR highlight your knowledge and experience with the skills that teachers need to possess. How do you answer if you haven't yet experienced the situation in a question? It is always important to remember that observations and student teaching are experience, and that you can answer a question based on what you observed another teacher doing. By answering in this manner, you indicated that you have seen the situation and will respond as the teacher you observed did. Another way to answer is to say that while you haven't actually experienced the situation yet, you have read of it or have studied it in a class. As you can tell by the nature of BBI questions, people who just walk in off the street really can't answer them. Hence, you should have confidence knowing that you have completed teacher-education training, have completed field experiences, and have received certification. A fully certified teacher is the best match to a job, so sell your preparation and certification, knowing that no teacher has experienced everything.

TELEPHONE SCREENING INTERVIEWS

The best hint to prepare for a telephone interview is to put a professional message on your answering machine or voice mail. Do not have a quirky, comical message that makes you sound like a college party animal instead of a teacher. What will a recruiter think if they call and hear, "Hey—you've reached me. If you are having a party, leave me a message. If not, hang up the phone so my true friends can call"?

A telephone interview is a preliminary interview and success in this format will net you an on-site interview. A phone interview often begins with some formalities, such as asking if you are still interested in the position, or asking if you have completed certification requirements since graduating. Most recruiters and interviewers who use phone interviews have prepared a list of a few questions that they ask each candidate. The interviewer is taking notes about what you say and rating each answer. The questions in a phone interview are considered sorting questions. Here are sample ones:

1. Tell me about your teaching experience.
2. Name one accomplishment from your previous teaching that characterizes your work.
3. Describe a typical lesson that you have taught.
4. In your cover letter, you mention _____. Describe what you learned from that experience.
5. Describe a classroom where you have taught, in terms of how it was organized.
6. Tell me about a positive classroom management experience that you have had.
7. What parts of your teacher education program helped you the most?
8. What else would you like to tell me about yourself with regard to your teaching experience?
9. Are you available to interview on _____?

You should answer each question using PAR or STAR to guide you. Since the interviewer cannot see your expressions, your answers and voice control are even more important. Time is of the essence in a phone interview, so remember to keep answers to 60 seconds. Be short and sweet!

Here are some good responses to "Tell me about your teaching experience":

1. In my teacher-education program at State University, I actually taught 10 lessons before student teaching, so I had experience with 2nd, 3rd, and 4th graders before my semester of student teaching. My placement in a 4th-grade classroom at Tyler Elementary in Collegetown was perfect, because I was able to teach all subjects. I was the lead teacher for three weeks, and I saw how much work goes into preparing students for the state tests every spring. I learned that 4th graders are almost middle schoolers, but they still need lots of practice and reinforcement in basic skills.

2. I completed student teaching with 7th- and 8th-grade math students at Model Middle School, and I learned that there are a lot of differences in their programs, their skill levels, and their individual growth. I was able to work with college-prep 8th graders who were very serious about getting ready for their high school college-prep courses, but I also experienced one 7th-grade remedial class. I learned that we need to accept students where they are, and then challenge them to learn more. They really need the skills that math has to offer and teaching with a variety of methods is the key.

When an employer asks about your experience, he or she wants to know the specific grade and subject levels, and the school and city. School and city tell the employer a lot about the demographics of the students with whom you have worked, so don't omit that. If you had any special field experiences, such as a two-week block in a school with predominantly non-English-speaking students, and the employer needs someone with this experience, mention it immediately. Again, you have to do your homework about each district where you apply, so that you can tailor your answers to their needs, indicating how your experiences and training are a match with their opening. Keep your answers short, but filled with pertinent information. If you keep a notebook with information about each district where you have applied, you can use that information in a phone interview. (Hint: Keep the notebook by the phone and have some written guidelines to help you answer. An outline of "talking points" can help you to sound more professional.)

Here's a good response to "Name one accomplishment from your previous teaching that characterizes your work":

I feel that I have really learned how to plan. I have planned lessons for three units that I taught, and it is indeed an accomplishment to complete a unit and have all students achieve at least a 75 percent on the unit test. My 3rd graders were able to do this on two math units and one language arts unit. While test scores aren't everything, I knew that they had learned the material through their test scores and my observations of their work.

What not to say:

> Well, I have indeed survived student teaching. I taught eight classes a day of exploratory Spanish to middle schoolers, and if I can do that, I think I can do anything. So my answer is that I can survive as a teacher.

What's the biggest difference in these two answers? The first answer is about student learning, and the teacher shows concern about his or her impact on their learning. The second answer is about survival. Teachers who are concerned about getting to the dismissal bell or getting to the last day of school seem to be thinking of themselves first, not their students.

More sample questions, with winning answers, will be covered in the following sections. Here are some more tips for telephone interviews:

1. When you know that employers may call, alert your family and/or housemates to be especially diplomatic when answering the phone. If they take messages for you, make sure that they deliver them to you.
2. If an employer leaves a message, call him or her back immediately. Your delay may lose you a job.
3. Some people list cell phone numbers as contact numbers. If you do this, be ready to take employer calls on your cell. If you are in heavy traffic, or the baby is screaming in the background, ask if you can call back at another time. Then call back when promised and make sure that there is no interruption at that time.
4. An interviewer may wish to record a call. Your permission must be given for this to occur, but doing so works in your favor. An employer who does this is probably doing so in order to review your answers a second time.
5. *Never* take another call while on the phone with an interviewer. *Never* seem too busy to take a call, unless it truly is an emergency.
6. *Always* be polite and thank the interviewer for his or her time.
7. A phone interview may only last 15 minutes and the employer may not offer you an on-site interview at the time. However, they may call back with the offer to interview in their district.

A few districts may send you an e-mail acknowledging their receipt of your cover letter and résumé. Their e-mail may instruct you to go to a website to complete their application or to complete a prerecorded phone interview.

(Teachers-teachers.com is a site used by some districts for this purpose.) The best advice is always the same: Do what the instructions say to do. If the e-mail contains some sorting questions, answer them in a timely manner, and use the spell-checker to make sure that your spelling doesn't cost you a job interview!

Once you have been offered an on-site interview, be sure to find out the following information:

1. Time and place of interview
2. Driving directions to the school, and parking availability
3. Who will conduct the interview
4. Any special requirements, such as teaching a mini-lesson, bringing a portfolio, or proof of citizenship/eligibility to work
5. A contact person at the interview site
6. The expected length of the interview

JOB FAIR INTERVIEWS

Consider interviewing at a job fair to be a little like speed dating—you have to make a good first impression, but you are also looking for a good match. Job fairs provide the opportunity to meet a large number of employers in a short amount of time. Employers who attend job fairs often pay to be there, so they want and need to meet strong candidates who can fill the jobs they have open. There are different locations for job fairs; some are held on your college's campus, others are held in school districts, and some may be located in civic centers or large hotels. Each job fair may have a slightly different venue.

One kind of fair is a recruitment fair where employers have booths advertising their openings, hoping to entice new graduates to move to their districts. At this kind of fair, look for signs advertising salary schedules, signing bonuses, and benefits of living in the district's community (picture beaches, or the bright lights of a big city to entice you). Districts may give you a pen, a CD describing their district, or a candy bar so that you remember who they are. These recruiters want a copy of your résumé and will encourage you to apply in their district after you leave the fair.

The second type of job fair is one where employers set up at tables and actually interview candidates. At this fair, you may have to stand in line for an interview, or you may sign up in advance for a time. Some fairs let candidates browse the employers' booths in the morning, then sign up for afternoon interviews.

How to Prepare for a Job Fair

As already mentioned, make sure you preregister for a fair if that is required. Read about the fair so that you know where it will be held, where you can park, and if there are any specific requirements of attendees. Some job fairs are now open only to fully certified teachers, so do not attempt to attend one of these fairs if you are just entering a teacher ed program or seeking an alternative route to certification.

Appropriate Clothes and Grooming

The old adage is still true—you only get one chance to make a first impression. Your clothing and grooming will make you stand out—in either a positive or negative way! What should you wear to a job fair? You should consider the fair a series of job interviews and wear your serious interview clothes. These are the same guidelines for on-site interviews.

For women:

1. A classic suit is always in style. The skirt should be knee length or longer, but not short. Dark colors or beige/tan are very appropriate. Many women choose a dark suit—navy, black, maroon, or gray—then wear a pastel shell or blouse with it.
2. A pants suit is appropriate, if it is tailored, and very professional. A pair of khakis and a blazer is not considered a pants suit. Whether you choose a suit with a skirt or tailored pants, your clothes must be neat, clean, pressed, and well-fitting.
3. Jewelry should be limited to what is considered "career" jewelry—a watch, one necklace, small earrings, and one ring per hand.
4. Shoes should be conservative heels or dressy flats and always well cleaned and polished. Do not wear high heels or shoes that are uncomfortable for walking, since job fairs are long days.

For men:

1. A classic dark suit with a white shirt and tie are always appropriate. Shirts may be beige or another light color if that matches the suit. Ties may have school buses or children or apples, too, because you are an educator.
2. Dark career shoes work well and should be cleaned and polished. No sneakers!
3. Jewelry should be limited to your watch and one ring per hand. Wearing earrings is a personal decision, but remember that many school districts are quite conservative.

For men and women:

1. While it sounds crazy to remind you of this, be clean and have clean hair and nails.
2. Your hair should be well-trimmed and styled—basically, not flamboyant.
3. If your job fair interview is after lunch, avoid spicy foods and use a mint!
4. Don't overuse a perfume, aftershave, or deodorant.
5. If you wear glasses, make sure that they are clean.
6. Do not have any alcoholic beverages before attending a job fair!
7. Do not chew gum when talking to recruiters at the fair.
8. No tobacco products before attending either—and don't leave the fair for a smoke outside. There are employers who will not hire anyone that they believe to be a smoker.

What to Bring to the Fair

You need to bring extra copies of your résumé to a job fair. Many recruiters are gathering résumés to decide whom they will interview later, and once a recruiter approves of how you look, your paperwork is the next deciding piece of the puzzle. Some people now bring interview portfolios with them. Your paperwork and portfolio should fit neatly into a small, manageable briefcase. Women should make the briefcase work as their purse, too, to avoid carrying so much stuff. Some candidates choose a nice notebook that holds their extra résumés instead of a briefcase. Make sure this notebook is professional looking, not a used one from former classes. You should carry paper and a pencil to write down notes and should be prepared to put district applications and business cards from recruiters somewhere.

To Get the Most From a Job Fair

1. Know the details of the fair from the beginning. Which districts will be interviewing? Can I actually interview for a specific position at the fair?
2. Research the districts that will be represented at the fair.
3. Make a plan of which districts you need to see at the fair and then plan your time accordingly.
4. After you meet with representatives at the fair, follow up by sending a cover letter and résumé to those contacts, even if they took a copy of your résumé. Write cover letters that are actually thank-you notes to the recruiters that interviewed you at the fair. The more recruiters see of your professionalism, the better your chances of getting an interview.

Job Fair Questions

At a job fair, interviews are typically 15 to 30 minutes long. Sometimes only three to five questions are asked of candidates. Job fair interview questions are very similar to telephone interview questions, since the interviewer is "sorting" candidates. First, interviewers will want the following from you:

1. Résumé
2. Complete name, contact information, and certification area, if not on résumé
3. The specifics of your certification area (When will your certification be complete and when will you be able to begin work?)
4. Your interest in special areas (coaching a sport, student council, honor society sponsor, tutoring, etc.) or your experience with special populations (ELL, high-risk students, etc.)

Once the interviewer sees that your certification is a match for the job opening, you will be asked a few basic questions. The interviewer will most probably be writing/evaluating your answers as you speak. Some interviewers enter their evaluations on a laptop at the fair, saving paper and rewrites on a form later. Don't be surprised by this.

1. Tell me about your experience teaching this grade and/or subject area.
2. Name one accomplishment from your previous teaching that characterizes your work.
3. If I had walked into your classroom in the past, describe what I would have seen.
4. Describe the components of a good lesson. How do you know it was a good one?
5. Tell me about a challenge or problem from your previous classroom experience that you resolved.

Will you be offered a job at a job fair? While some fairs offer letters of intent and even contracts at fairs, most job fair interviews are just preliminary. At the end of your interview, the recruiter will thank you for interviewing and inform you of their timeline. They may request that you go to their website and complete their online application, or that you mail them official transcripts and a paper application. Whatever they request, do it—and complete their requests in a timely manner.

If you are a fully certified teacher in a high-needs field—such as math, science, foreign languages, ELL, or special education—you may be offered a contract. Unless you have researched this district and know with absolute certainty that this job is the perfect one, don't sign that day. Graciously accept the paperwork and ask about the deadline for a response. If you are still unsure, ask if you may visit their district for an on-site interview. If they are truly recruiting you, they should be able to give you up to a week to respond, and they should be happy to schedule an on-site interview.

Many times job fair interviews end with an invitation to interview on-site, or at least a timeline of when on-site interviews will take place. Your follow-up to the job fair interview may make the final decision in the interviewer's mind about whether you merit that on-site interview. Always follow up if you want the job. Send the thank-you note to the person with whom you interviewed, and send all requested paperwork to the designated offices. Now, you are ready for an on-site interview.

THE ALL-IMPORTANT ON-SITE INTERVIEW

The on-site interview remains the most frequently used mechanism for hiring new teachers. You can psych yourself up for an interview by remembering that the employer needs a teacher to fill the position that is open. No principal wants to start the new school year without enough teachers! Additionally, you are a top contender or you wouldn't have gotten the interview. So—be confident!

In the on-site interview, you have the opportunity to let the employer see how well you present yourself, how articulate you are, and above all, how much you know about the skills of teaching. All of your research about the district will pay off in the on-site interview. So will your efforts to look your best. A few preliminary reminders include:

1. Find out with whom you are interviewing. It is often a personnel director and a building principal. It may be just one person for the whole interview. It may be a committee that includes the principal and other teachers of that grade/subject. The more you know before the interview, the less apt you are to feel surprised and unsettled.
2. Always arrive on time, or a few minutes early. Arriving late is disastrous, as you are rushed, and it's a black mark against you.
3. Always dress professionally, as described in the specifics for dressing for job fairs. There is no excuse for not wearing career clothes that are neat and pressed.
4. Bring paper and pencil, your interview portfolio, and any other specific paperwork requested.

5. Do not schedule anything else immediately after the interview, as the interviewer may invite you to a faculty meeting or to meet some other teachers, lengthening the interview. Never seem too busy to interview. Having to leave for childcare reasons is a *big* mark against you, as it indicates you don't have your childcare situation well organized. (Past behavior predicts future performance.)
6. Initial impressions are important. Smile. Seem happy to be there. Have a good, solid handshake.
7. Be nice to *everyone*. This is especially true of secretaries, support staff, and custodians. No one will hire a candidate if the secretary reports that he or she was rude or condescending upon arrival in the office.
8. Know where to park and *never* take a reserved spot.
9. Act calm. Don't talk on your cell phone while waiting for the office. Turn it off and *never* take a call or even let the phone ring during an interview. Again, what you do predicts future performance. If you say you have to have the cell on to take a call from your spouse, then the principal knows you will take a lot of calls while trying to teach. It's over right there for you.
10. No slouching or bored body language! If you are not enthused and energetic at the interview, it can be predicted that you really won't be if hired.

Be prepared for an interviewer to read questions from a prepared list, or at least to refer to it. Answer succinctly, using PAR and STAR to guide your answers. Allow the interviewer time to record answers and evaluations. Do not ask to see his or her notes or evaluations. This is simply not done.

So, what does a typical interview look like? You arrive at least 10 minutes before the interview is to begin and introduce yourself to a receptionist/secretary/office support staff person. You are seated and wait. If there is information on the table about the district—pick it up and skim it. The interviewer greets you and you shake hands. Upon entering the office or conference room, introductions of other interviewers are made. Shake hands with each and sit when invited to do so.

The interviewer generally outlines the building/district interview schedule and then begins. Some interviewers use icebreaker questions such as "Tell me about yourself" or "What events brought you to my office today?" or "In your cover letter, you mentioned _____. Tell me more about that." Another common icebreaker question is, "Tell me one thing that is not on your résumé that you want me to know." No matter how the question is posed, remember two things: 1) a 60-second answer is about all the interviewer will listen to, so be succinct, and 2) give a behavior-based answer.

Question: What events brought you to my office today?
Answer: I am completing my bachelor's degree in biology with full teacher certification in May, and I am in the process of completing student teaching at Rockton High School. Student teaching has shown me that teaching really is the right profession for me, because I love helping students learn. I want to teach life sciences at all high school levels, and I'd love to coach baseball, too.

Question: Tell me one thing that is not on your résumé that you want me to know.
Answer: My résumé doesn't indicate why I am so interested in your district. When I was in middle school, we competed with this middle school in chorus, and I still remember how outstanding the program was. I want to be a part of a school music program that offers students the opportunities to sing and perform in many venues. Your middle school program still has its great reputation and I want to be a part of it—helping students every step of the way.

After the icebreaker questions come the nuts-and-bolts ones. These questions should be the same for every candidate. Examples are given in the next chapter and in the appendix.

Be Ready to Ask Some Questions

After asking questions, interviewers say, "What questions do you have of us?" You should definitely have some questions. If something specific has not been made clear, ask it. You may ask about assignments, typical class sizes, and the availability of a classroom of your own. (Do not assume you will have a room of your own if this is not stated. Many new teachers share rooms and float until they have more seniority.) At the elementary level, you may ask if paraprofessionals are used in classes at the school. Do not ask a question that is already answered on the school or district website, such as the mission or enrollment numbers. Other pertinent questions include:

1. I am interested in participating in an induction/mentoring program. Can you describe the one here?
2. What professional development opportunities are available for teachers here?
3. What types of technology are available in the classroom?
4. Anything specific about the school that indicates you have some knowledge, and are genuinely interested in learning more.
5. How would you describe the support from parents in this community?

Do not ask all of these questions. Pick one as your standard question to ask, and use it if a better one does not come along.

At the very end of an interview, the interviewer will explain when the hiring decisions will be made and how candidates are contacted about decisions. Salary schedules are discussed briefly in interviews, as are benefits. The interviewer may just give you a handout of these and refer you to the website.

You usually know when an interview is over because the interviewer stands up! Shake hands again and be cordial and enthusiastic when leaving. If an interviewer asks, "If we were to offer you this position, would you take it?" be ready with some response. You should say the truth, but worded very diplomatically.

Examples:

"I am even more interested in this position than before the interview, so yes, I am very interested in being a teacher here."

"I've learned a lot today and I remain interested in the position. If you were to offer me the position, I would need a few days to discuss it with my family, but yes, I am very interested."

Most employers know that you want to discuss any offer with your significant others. Of course, if this job is "the one," go ahead and say, "Yes, absolutely, if you offer me this position, I will accept." Try not to be negative. Some employers will list candidates in order of how excited they seem about coming to work in their school, if all other factors are equal. When an employer asks, "If we were to offer you this position, would you take it?" and you answer, "I'm very unsure because of _____," you can bet your name just went to the bottom of the list. If you say, "No, I just don't think this is the job for me," it's all over, too. Additionally, the interviewer will tell every principal in his or her district that you are just not adaptable. If you don't want the job, then say "no" directly and thank the employer for the interview, explaining that the information you learned today was very valuable. Next time, do a little more research about the job before applying.

Illegal Questions

No matter where you interview in the United States, federal laws guide the questions that can and cannot be asked in an interview. You may not be asked questions about your gender, race, color, national origin, religion, age, or disabilities. Not only does the interviewer have to adhere to these federal guidelines, but so must the support staff and anyone with whom you have contact during an interview. For example, if you were waiting in a dentist's office, a stranger might strike up a conversation with you about seeing you last week in her church. You start to talk and she asks if you have a family, and so forth. It is illegal for the secretary of the school to have the same conversation with you.

There are nuances to asking illegal questions. An interviewer is not sup-posed to say, "What a pretty ring. Tell me about it." Your ring might indicate marriage or religious background. Asking "How long have you lived here?" is an illegal question if the employer is trying to ascertain if you are an im-migrant to the country. Nontraditional new teachers may be in their 40s or 50s, and it is illegal for the interviewer to try to ascertain their exact age by asking, "When did you graduate from high school?" The truth is, your tran-script probably has your date of birth, but the employer cannot ask about it.

But what should you do if you are asked an illegal question? You may an-swer it politely and move on, or you can answer it indirectly and refer back to your teaching skills. When asked about her children, one candidate re-sponded, "I can honestly say that raising my own children has given me a lot of insight into teaching. I remember how my son struggled with math in 3rd grade and because of that I can relate to other students who struggle. Let me explain how I have helped those who struggle with math. . . ."

Hopefully, you will only be asked pertinent questions in the interview that relate to your skills, background, and experience in teaching. Even if a ques-tion is not worded in the style of a behavior-based one, you can always an-swer with a response that describes your skills and teaching experience.

Using an Interview to See if *You* Want to Work *There*

You are not the only one being interviewed when you visit a school. You are also interviewing the potential employer, colleagues, and staff to determine if *you* want to work *there*. Before you go the interview, read the website and talk with your professors or other teachers who might know the school's reputa-tion. When you are on-site, consider the following:

1. Is the school in a safe area? If not, are there signs of safety features, such as a resource officer, metal detectors, and easy access to adults in the main office?
2. Is the school clean? Look for clean floors, restrooms, windows, and a lack of graffiti and trash.
3. Are front office staff cordial and effective? Are you welcomed by the interviewer, or does he or she seem too busy to interview you?
4. Do the teachers seem positive, or stressed out?
5. Are the room assignments, class size, and course load clearly ex-plained? Are these factors "doable"? Can I accept this job and achieve success, or will the load and class size be an impossible position?
6. Why is this opening available? Has another teacher left? Are enroll-ments increasing? Did low-achieving, unmotivated students drive off the last teacher?

7. Will I have extra- or cocurricular duties, such as a lunchroom supervision, or after-school programs? Will I have to coach or sponsor a significant activity to get this job, or do they really want a "teacher?"
8. Will the administration that hires me still be here next year? What are administrative and teacher turnover rates?
9. Does my philosophy of teaching match this school's? Do the methods I want to use match the ones used here? (If a school uses prepackaged curricula, and you don't believe in teaching with a script that someone else wrote, that's a bad match!)
10. Does the salary this district offers allow me to live in this community? Comparing cost of living to salary can be very important.

An Interesting Story

A new teacher went to an on-site interview where the principal spoke with her for only a few minutes, then took a call. She was interrupted several times by the office staff with "crisis" questions, and then she took another call. When the candidate returned to campus to discuss the interview with her professor, she said, "If this is how I'm treated there when they are trying to recruit me, how much attention will I get as a teacher? I don't think this is the place for me."

Another teacher returned to campus with this tale of interview woe: "The principal ended the interview by saying that I shouldn't feel bad if they didn't hire me, because their number-one candidate was an applicant from an ivy league school. Quite frankly, that was just rude. I do not want to work for someone who doesn't know anything about personnel management."

To summarize, interviewing is a two-way street. The school strives to hire the best new teachers and candidates need to decide if the work environment of the school is a good match for them. The more information-rich an interview is, the more you will know about the position. People who stay in jobs tend to be ones whose expectations are met, so the most important thing to learn in an interview is the exact job description and expectations. If the employer says you will have a 2nd-grade class of about 20 students and they will be a mix of ability levels, but then you discover that you are really assigned a group of 27 and 14 of them are in the diagnosis process for special education, your expectations have not been met. If you are told that you will have up to 30 in a class and that up to half of them will be special needs students, and you agree to that challenge, you will feel that you have chosen the job that you wanted. Look for a school that practices "truth in advertising" and that tells you everything up front. The best scenario is no surprises. Now, let's get back to how you get the job by giving the very best answers.

5

The Interview Questions and Answers

This chapter presents three to five sample questions for each of the following areas of teaching competencies, along with sample answers.

1. Curriculum (what is taught/meeting state-mandated standards)
2. Planning and methods (how we teach)
3. Classroom management and discipline
4. How to assess, evaluate, and grade student work
5. Student motivation (how students learn/developmental readiness)
6. Meeting the needs of diverse students, including special education, gifted, and English-language learners
7. Communication with parents, colleagues, and administrators
8. Professional issues

The answers are provided as a starting point. Obviously, you can't memorize these answers and hope that an interviewer asks one of the questions for which you have memorized an answer. Rather, read the answers to gain ideas for your answers. Remember to use STAR and PAR to guide how you answer. Interviewers want to know if you have the background, experience, and skills to do the job of teaching. You need to sell your past education, field experiences, and your teacher certification. Always strive to be succinct and tell an example to make a point.

If something in a sample answer sounds totally unfamiliar to you, you may want to read a book or do some follow-up to find out more about the topic. Lots of information is available on the Web, as well.

Appendix A of this book lists questions for specific grade and subject levels, as well as for special education, and questions for those who may be entering teaching with no previous teaching background. To be prepared for any interview, read this chapter, then go to Appendix A for specific questions about the grade/subject you plan to teach.

Some answers are in the first person, indicating that this is how a candidate would word the answer, although these are *not* actual candidate answers used by anyone. The other answers are hints and strategies on how to formulate an answer.

CURRICULUM

1. Tell Me About the Most Important Parts of the Curriculum for This Grade/Subject.

Answer: Your answer should begin by noting that there are state curriculum guidelines, and that you are familiar with them because you used them to guide your teaching in a field experience. Next, give a specific example, such as building reading skills in lower elementary school, or math topics for upper and middle grades. If you teach high school, give specific curriculum topics that are taught universally throughout your state, such as literature, writing, or a specific social studies unit.

Portfolio hint: You may show a unit that you used in student teaching when asked this question, then briefly explain how the unit met state- and district-mandated curriculum standards.

2. Describe Your Experiences Teaching _____ (Reading, Advanced Math, Science, Whatever the Subject Content Is for the Grade[s] You Will Teach).

Answer: Be specific in your answer about the curriculum taught. For example, "In teaching reading, I have learned to use a balanced approach. My classes read big books when I introduce something new, but I always incorporate phonics, spelling, and vocabulary into every lesson. I make use of a word wall, and there are spelling tests at this level. I want my students to be prepared for the standardized tests, but more importantly, I want them to love to read for themselves."

Tip: When asked about curriculum, think about a favorite textbook that you have used. What are the big topics in the book? These topics were probably chosen because they met the state curriculum. While a textbook is never the whole curriculum, it is a starting point and a guide.

3. Teachers Often Say That There Is Too Much to Teach. What Have You Learned That Must Always Be in the Curriculum for This Grade/Subject Area?

Answer: In teaching Spanish, I know that every class must include listening, speaking, reading, and writing. I create my lessons around the topics from the state curriculum, like greetings, food vocabulary, geography, clothing, and so forth, but I make sure that students actually do the four skills each day. After all, the students need to know how to listen to Spanish, speak it, read it, and write it if they are to actually use it in the real world.

4. There Is So Much to Teach. How Do You Break the Curriculum Down Into Manageable Divisions?

Answer: Curriculum becomes manageable when teachers have multiple layers of planning. For instance, the use of curriculum mapping helps teachers to see the big content topics that will be taught throughout the year. Unit planning helps teachers organize bigger chunks of the material to cover in one- to two-week time frames. Of course, lesson planning is essential. Talk about how you have done some of this planning, and talk about how you have planned with colleagues to further impress the interviewer.

Tip: If you are not familiar with curriculum mapping, read the books by Heidi Hayes Jacobs listed in the bibliography.

PLANNING AND METHODS (HOW WE TEACH)

1. How Have You Planned Lessons That Work for This Age/Grade Level?

Answer a: A good plan is like a good speech, it has an introduction, a body, and a conclusion. As a teacher, I have to get the students' attention and get them focused before I can start teaching. The body of my lesson plan will indicate what I do and what the students do, with a lot of variety. The conclusion should include some assessment, since I need to know if they have learned what I taught. Let me show you a plan. (And then you open your portfolio to a good, clear one-page lesson plan, which you summarize quickly.)

Answer b: (You open your portfolio to a lesson plan that you have written.) This plan is typical of what I did in student teaching. Since I had five classes a day of 7th graders, I didn't dare not plan. This plan started with a warm-up, review activity. Then I introduced the new topic, our state's entrance into the union, with a guided outline, so that they had to write. I had students do a short, small-group activity about what we would name our state if we were naming it. I timed the activity and enforced my rule that they had to justify their name based on a historical fact. There was a three-question quiz at the end. That class just flew by and students liked it. The only thing I would change would be to do that activity closer to our field trip to the state capitol.

2. Tell Me About a Plan That Didn't Work and What Might Have Made It Successful.

Answer: In student teaching, I taught a lesson on paragraph writing that did not work out at all the way I thought it would. I had a plan, with all the steps written down to lead students through the paragraph-writing activity, but I hadn't thought about their lack of basic skills before I started teaching the lesson. I realized immediately that their thesis statement sentences weren't even sentences in a few cases. I guess I made the classic mistake of thinking that they had already mastered how to write a sentence. So, during the lesson, I had to teach a mini-lesson about how to write a great sentence. When I teach this next time, I will be sure to make my review about writing sentences. When I know that they can do that, then we'll start paragraphs. I've learned that a little assessment up front can help a lot!

3. What Are Some of Your Favorite Ways to Begin and End Classes?

Answer: My students know that there is a procedure for coming into class, putting their book bags in their cubbies, sitting down at their tables, and getting out the supplies that are on the model table/desk. I usually have a paper to return to them, with a smiley face or sticker, and they know to read whatever is on their desk. It is so calming to have this routine! At the end of the day, we have our set of procedures, too. I actually keep a laminated poster of how we straighten our desks and tables, gather our book bags, and then sit until we get the final "what we learned today" phrase or vocabulary word. The students are supposed to tell me what they learned and liked about class that day, then say good-bye at the door as they go to their rides. Third graders still need so much guidance. I would have these kinds of procedures for any grade, though.

Tip: If you haven't learned how to teach procedures, read the Harry K. Wong book listed in the bibliography. The best teachers use his methods, and principals love to hear that you have read his book and can implement procedures.

4. What Are Some of the Methods You Have Used to Teach _____?

Answer: The answer to this question varies widely according to grade and subject areas. Some tried-and-true methods include teaching by modeling, teaching with questions, using visuals, cooperative learning groups, and so forth. Review your methods textbook from your college classes, or read *A Handbook for Classroom Instruction that Works* by R.J. Marzano et al., or *First Time in the High School Classroom* by M.C. Clement, which are both listed in the bibliography. When you do answer this question, describe a method that you have used and that has worked well. Remember to follow PAR or STAR. Never answer this question by saying that you just stand up and lecture to students—even if they are in high school!

5. How Have You Integrated Technology Into Your Lessons?

Answer: If you are lucky enough to have had experience where you could teach lessons using the Internet in your room, or could take students to a computer lab, describe how this worked for you. If your past experiences were in schools that didn't necessarily offer a lot of technology, then talk about how you use the Internet to search for more teaching ideas, how technology has simplified how you create quizzes and tests, or how you have guided students to do research on computers in the library.

CLASSROOM MANAGEMENT AND DISCIPLINE

1. What Steps Have You Taken or Observed in the Past to Create Positive Classroom Management?

Answer: Good classroom management begins with a plan. In student teaching, my teacher and I used a plan with rules, positive reinforcements, and corrective actions. There were only four rules, and they were observable and enforceable by us. The rules made sense. We taught the rules the first two weeks of school and reviewed them on the days after long breaks. We sent a letter home about our plan, and parents signed it. Here is a copy of the plan, and I have a copy of the letter, too. I would start my classroom this fall with the same type of plan that I learned to use in student teaching.

Portfolio hint: Use the classroom management plan in your portfolio as a visual aide when answering this question.

2. If I Had Visited One of the Classrooms Where You Taught, What Would I Have Seen That Evidences Good Classroom Management?

Answer: For starters, there is always an assignment on the board for students to work on when they get to class. I greet students at the door, trying to say something personal to each one as they enter. While they are settling and working on the thought question, I take attendance quickly, with a seating chart, not by calling out names. I also have an agenda of what we will do on the board. Students know to look ahead to the agenda if they finish early. All of these procedures, combined with a classroom management plan that is posted on the wall, provide the parameters for keeping students on task. Also, and very importantly, my room is arranged so that I can walk around the desks. Teachers have to monitor all the time, and not from behind a desk. With all this in place—not only can I teach, but I can smile before Christmas!

3. What Kinds of Things Actually Reward Students This Age? What Kinds of Things Are Effective Consequences?

Answer: This answer varies greatly depending on the age of the student. For 1st graders, having lunch with the teacher can be a great positive reinforcement for good behavior. However, for a 9th grader, lunch with the teacher might be the worst punishment imaginable. The best rewards for good behavior involve academic extras, like letting the student pick a book to read, or having a student get to use the computer or go to a learning center. Some consequences do not need to be severe to be effective. For example, staying one minute after class for a mini-conference with the teacher can be very effective. See the books by the Canters and by Fred Jones in the bibliography for more specific ideas.

Another hint to include in this answer: Classroom management is all about how the teacher organizes time, students, materials, and space in the room. Yes, a management plan is important, but a classroom can't be "managed" by strict rules where every little response either gets a piece of candy or a correction. Look for best practices in management and discipline in the schools where you observe and prepare carefully for questions about management. They will always be included in interviews, because management issues drive many new teachers out of their jobs every year. Every principal needs to know that you can manage a classroom successfully. This may be even more important than what and how you teach, because, without effective management, you won't get the chance to teach the curriculum.

4. Describe a Common Misbehavior for Students and What You Have Done in the Past to Correct That Behavior.

Answer a: Talking is a constant issue for middle school students. They want to talk to each other about everything and when we discuss, they want to blurt out answers. I have found that I need to use talking as a reward. I often say, "If the majority of the class gets the assignment done, then the class earns three talk-time minutes." To resolve the blurting out problem, I ask a question and give 20 seconds of think time. Then I get better answers, too. Of course, I had to put a little work into teaching this procedure. Overall, there are certainly misbehaviors that we can redirect into positive behaviors. As teachers, we have to remember that we teach behavior, as well as academics, and doing so will hopefully raise achievement.

Answer b: Go back to PAR and think of one specific misbehavior that you have seen out in schools. State the misbehavior (problem) and the action that you have taken or would take to improve the behavior. State the intended result. Reassure the interviewer that you have worked with real students and know that they do not automatically behave, but when taught procedures and routines, backed up by a management plan, student behaviors can be improved.

5. Describe a Time When a Student Questioned Your Authority or When a Student Broke a Class Rule and How You Responded.

Answer a: In field experiences, students constantly question the authority of the student teacher, especially if he or she is my age—just 22. I found that it helped to dress professionally, be overprepared for the lessons, and to be sure and know the school and classroom policies. As a new teacher, I plan to do the same. I also plan to talk with a mentor, or just another teacher down the hall, to make sure that I always know the policies before the students start to challenge me.

Answer b: One of the most important things that I have learned about classroom rules is that students will test the teacher to make sure that he or she actually means business. I know that if I have a rule with a posted consequence, then I have to enforce that consequence. With one student last semester, I used the broken record technique when he said I couldn't give him a detention. I simply said, "You have chosen to break rule two and by doing so, you have chosen a detention. If you break another rule, you will be choosing another detention." He started to fight back with more words, and I just said my line again. I started teaching again and he got the message.

HOW TO ASSESS, EVALUATE, AND GRADE STUDENT WORK

1. While You Are Teaching, How Can You Tell If Students Are "Getting" the Material?

Answer a: I like to stop and do "think, pair, and share" questions throughout my lessons. I ask a fairly tough question, give 30 to 60 seconds to think with a partner, and then ask for answers. I can assess the verbal answers to decide if I need to reinforce a concept or even reteach a topic. Getting instant feedback helps me teach, and making students answer keeps them on task. It's a formative assessment—no grade—just feedback for me.

Answer b: When students are working on an assignment, that's when I'm not only helping them, but assessing what they know and where they are having trouble. I'm constantly walking around, checking answers, and asking, "How did you get that answer?" If students can explain the procedures, then they are truly understanding math.

2. Describe Your Grading System to Me As If I Were Your Class. In Other Words, How Will I Be Graded in Your Class?

Answer: Grades should not be surprises, to parents or to students. In my classes, I use a total point system. Every homework assignment counts 5 to 10 points; quizzes count 15 to 35 points; chapter tests are 50 to 120 points; if there are special projects, then they count 30 to 50 points. I keep track of total points and just divide points earned by possible points for a percentage. In my student teaching, the school set the grading scale of 92 percent for an A, 84 percent for a B, 75 percent for a C, and 68 percent as a D. Of course, each school or department may set its own minimum for a letter grade. I can average a student's grade at any time, and the students can track their own grades. It is so fair and I found it has worked well. It's an easy system to teach students, too.

Hint: Open your portfolio to a one-page explanation of your grading scale, or a sample letter that you have sent home to parents explaining how grades are determined.

3. Homework Has Become a Much-Debated Subject. How Have You Used Homework and How Have You Evaluated Students' Homework?

Answer: Homework can be a valuable tool to reinforce student learning. It can help students practice a skill until it becomes automatic. Outside reading as homework helps us to cover more in class. If I give homework, I always do something with it. Sometimes I have students check their own papers with answers on the overhead screen or board. Other times I spot check homework to see if it is done, and then I give 0 to 5 points for completion. If the homework will help me to assess their learning, then I do collect and grade it. By telling students that I will do this randomly, then following through with what I've said, they should be motivated to do their homework. Through homework, I can catch a student who is not having success long before a major test.

STUDENT MOTIVATION (HOW STUDENTS LEARN/DEVELOPMENTAL READINESS)

1. How Have You Motivated or Encouraged Students to Achieve Their Highest Potential?

Answer: This is truly a tough question for any new or veteran teacher to answer. A good answer might begin with an explanation of how you have applied something from an educational psychology class to your teaching. For example, we know that students who are hungry or scared or who don't know whose house they will return to after school are not "ready" to learn because their other basic needs aren't being met. Helping these children get into a breakfast program, or into counseling, may be the first step in motivating them to learn.

Additionally, the answer to this will vary greatly from one grade level to another. Putting pictures of freshmen on a bulletin board labeled, "The graduating class of 20__" may motivate some to think they can actually graduate. Cheering students at their sports events may motivate them to work a little harder back in your classroom. Celebrating success by writing private comments on papers and perhaps sending notes home may motivate some students. The true answer to this is that different things motivate different students. The teacher has to know the students and their needs before knowing how to motivate them. Lastly, if you have experienced a specific incident where you motivated a student, repeat that vignette here for the interviewer.

2. Describe an Activity That Would Bore a Student Who Was Older and Frustrate a Student Who Was Younger Than This Grade Level. In Other Words, What Activities Are Developmentally Appropriate for This Grade Level?

Answer: Again, there will be much variation here, but think of specific skills that you could describe. For elementary-aged children, you can discuss some eye-hand coordination issues that might affect handwriting. At the high school level, students may not be mature enough for the explicit topics of some novels, even though they have the reading levels to read the novel. You can share your knowledge of constructivist teaching here, talking about getting students into their "zones of proximal development," where they are challenged by new material, but not so overwhelmed that they shut down and say, "I can't."

3. Describe an Activity or Lesson Where the Students Themselves Said That They Loved Learning the Material. Why Do You Think They Enjoyed It So Much?

Answer: This is your chance to let the interviewer know that you know how children learn best. Talk about how students learn by doing, by experiencing, and by practicing. Describe a lesson that you taught that was successful and describe how you got student feedback about your teaching.

4. How Have You Handled Students Who Say, "I Can't Do That," or Who Quit Doing Any Work in Class?

Answer: In student teaching, I saw some middle school students who did this. When I asked my cooperating teacher for help, she always suggested that I find out more about the student by talking with the counselor or the student support team members. With one student, we developed an individual contract for work that he and his mother signed. When he reverted to his "do-nothing" mode, we called home. When he did assignments, he got extra computer time, which he liked. We also let him type some assignments on the computer, instead of write, which he did. In his case, we had to really push, get parent support, and try the computer angle. It worked. If we had let him do nothing, he would have failed 7th grade. He passed with a C average because we individualized for him and pushed him.

MEETING THE NEEDS OF DIVERSE STUDENTS

Since diversity includes many categories—gifted, special education, and English-language learners (ELLs)—the interviewer will design these questions based on the specific needs of the school district. The better you have researched the demographics of the district, the better you will be able to anticipate these questions. Much information about a district is available on its website.

1. Describe an Experience You Have Had Teaching Special Education Students in the Regular Classroom.

Answer: If you had this experience, describe it. Interviewers are looking for examples of how you collaborated with the specialists who came into the classroom to work with these students, or how you worked with the specialists who pulled students out of your classroom. The most prevalent current model is to actually have two teachers in a classroom of elementary students, one regular teacher, or "teacher of record," and the specialist. A good answer to this question would include your experiences team teaching with a special education teacher. If you haven't had this experience, you can describe team teaching with an ELL teacher or a teacher of gifted students.

2. How Have You Modified Lessons or Assignments for English-Language Learners or Special Education Students?

Answer a: My best strategy for ELL students is to be very visual. Even if I say "page 42," then I know I need to write a 42 on the board. While I don't speak Spanish, I learned just a few phrases, such as "favor de abrir los libros," which means "please open your books." It really helps.

Answer b: With regard to modifying assignments, I have learned to use a lot of outlines for helping students. While some students can copy notes onto a blank outline, special education students need more of the notes given to them, with just some blanks to fill in. This strategy can help ELL students, too.

There are many strategies for helping students. Remember that not all special needs students are diagnosed, and that you will have academically diverse students in one classroom. An 11th-grade English teacher who discovers that some of her students have 2nd-grade reading levels has to learn to adapt lessons and individualize reading assignments based on this academic diversity.

3. How Have You Found Back-Up Help for a Student Problem If You Felt the Concern Was Beyond Your Area of Expertise?

Answer: The nice part of student teaching was having a mentor in the room all the time who knew the students. As a new teacher, I would ask my assigned mentor questions as they arose, just as I asked my cooperating teacher in the past. I would also turn to the lead grade-level teacher or department chair. In schools, there are always resource people, and I would get to know them. Counselors, nurses, school psychologists, and administrators can help me find help for my students.

For example, in student teaching I asked my cooperating teacher if she felt that I should tutor one of our students. She suggested that I refer him to the peer-tutoring program as a first step. I didn't even know about the program, but once we got the student into the after-school sessions, his class work really improved.

COMMUNICATION WITH PARENTS, COLLEAGUES, AND ADMINISTRATORS

1. Describe Positive Parent Communications That You Have Used in the Past.

Answer: At the beginning of my student teaching semester, I wrote a letter of introduction to the parents of my students. I told them how pleased I was to have the opportunity to work with their students, and I described the next unit we would do together in the class. I also added calendar reminders about the upcoming state testing dates. I included my e-mail address if they had questions or comments. As a full-time teacher, I plan to do a letter like this at the beginning of every nine-week grading period.

Hint: Show a letter that you used in a field experience from your portfolio as you talk. Even if you didn't use a letter in your field experience, show a sample letter that you would send home that explains your management plan or your grading plan. Employers want to know that you see the value of communication with students' families.

2. Tell About a Time When You Discussed an Issue With a Parent and Then the Student's Behavior or Academic Progress Changed.

Answer: In student teaching we had parent/student/teacher conferences at the middle school. At one conference, a student's mother attended with her daughter, and the daughter was to show some of her work to her mother, explaining what she learned. At one point, the mother stopped her daughter and said, "I honestly can't read your handwriting. I guess I haven't seen your writing in a while." As teachers, we knew about the handwriting and spelling problems that the student was having but hadn't received any support from the mother for the girl to go to a special class during homeroom for some diagnostic tests. After that three-way conference, the mother saw her daughter's needs and asked us if we could help. We immediately described the testing program and help that could come from the special homeroom class. The mother agreed to the testing. It's too bad the daughter hadn't received help much earlier, but sometimes it takes something this dramatic to show the parents the need that exists.

3. Has a Parent or Guardian Ever Confronted You About a Student's Achievement or Contested an Assignment? If So, What Did You Do to Resolve the Conflict?

Answer: While it wasn't a huge confrontation, I did have a parent call the school and ask why her child's grades went down when I started teaching the class as a student teacher. My teacher and I were told of the call and we attempted to call the parent back. There was no response, so my teacher and I wrote a letter, explaining the grading scale and listing her child's scores for the nine weeks. When the parent saw that her child had quit doing homework, she called us directly, and together we explained that if her son would start turning in homework again, his average would definitely improve. We found out that her son had just started a part-time job, and had told his mother that he was doing well with the regular teacher, but he thought the tests were harder when I gave them. Our direct communication, showing the zeros for homework scores, indicated a different story. He started turning in homework again. The clearer the lines of communication from the school to the families can be, the better.

4. Tell About Your Most Positive Experience Team Teaching or Working With Your Colleagues on a Team or Committee.

Answer a: In my junior year practicum experience, I worked with another junior and we co-taught a unit on historical novels from the Civil War. She was the novel expert and I was the history expert. Our mentor teachers had done this unit before, and they helped us block out enough time to cover all the material. I learned that brainstorming and lesson planning with another person can be a really good idea, and that when students see teachers making connections from one subject to another, they tend to remember those topics better. Not only did we get As for our unit, but I think that the students really learned more.

Answer b: While I haven't had a chance to team teach, I have worked on a lot of committees at my college sorority. I served as the vice-president of my sorority, and in that position I chaired the rush/interview committee. Together with five other women, we organized three interview weekends and had a total of 178 women interview in person for the house. After all the interviews, I led the meeting to determine which 24 women would get invitations to live with us. The timeline that the committee made, and the outlines that we determined we would use, helped us to achieve the goal. I would use the same types of strategies for working with other teachers to plan any big event or to simply sit down and organize the units of the semester.

Hint: If you have had no experience with the topic in the question as a teacher, you can explain your experience with a similar issue from college or a summer job. If those experiences don't fit, then go back to your own years as a student and tell about something that you observed your former teachers do. "I still remember how my 9th-grade history and English teachers collaborated so that we read the literature that accompanied each historic period we studied. It really made a difference in how we learned. My high school math and science teachers did some joint planning, too, so that we knew the mathematics that we needed to know to get through the science classes." By recognizing how well this worked when you were a student, you are at least telling the interviewer that you are aware of what can be done by effective teachers.

PROFESSIONAL ISSUES

1. How Have You Evaluated Your Teaching?

Answer: We had a lot of observations during student teaching. Additionally, I videotaped two lessons and wrote self-evaluations of those lessons. At the end of one of my units, I had the students complete an evaluation of that unit. It was intended to give me feedback, and I asked questions such as "Which lesson from the unit on insects helped you learn the most?" and "If you were teaching this science unit, is there any activity that you would leave out?" Getting students to tell how they learned and what helped them to learn is a valuable tool. There are always a few who don't take it seriously, but if student input is requested on an ongoing basis, they tend to be honest and helpful. It's an empowerment thing for them.

2. How Do You Stay Current in the Trends and Issues in Education and in Your Subject-Matter Field(s)?

Answer: Your answer should indicate that you maintain at least one or two professional memberships. For the field of education, maintaining a membership in Kappa Delta Pi, an international honor society in education, or Phi Delta Kappa, and reading their journals will keep you informed on all the top issues. Additionally, being an active member in one of the professional associations for your subject field and attending state or national conferences will help you stay current. After all, would you want to visit a physician who didn't read a medical journal after graduation?

Another way to answer this question is to describe any professional development workshops you have recently completed, or to discuss with the interviewer how you plan to complete your master's degree. In some states you must complete a minimum number of hours of continuing education to keep your teaching credentials valid. You may choose to answer this question by explaining how you will complete the continuing education course work to keep your teaching license valid.

3. What Parts of Your Teacher Education Program Have Helped You the Most?

Answer: Most graduates report that student teaching was the most valuable part of their teacher education program, so this is a very safe answer. If you say this, however, you should support it with some evidence. "In student teaching I learned how to apply all the theories, techniques, and methods I learned on campus in a real classroom. Having an excellent cooperating teacher made the experience even better, because she could explain why and how she did certain things. She let me use her plans and ideas at first, and then she helped me to plan on my own. By the end of the semester, she was my mentor and sometimes my co-teacher. It was a good experience."

What *not* to say: The classes didn't really help us learn. After all, the real teachers who supervised our student teaching said that they didn't learn anything in classes either. The best way to learn to teach is just to jump in. The seminars that accompanied student teaching were so boring. We all just sat there and got our points for being there, but we didn't learn a thing.

Remember that past behavior is the best predictor of future performance. If you talk about boring professors or boring classes or seminars on campus, that is a predictor that you will find faculty meetings and teacher in-service/professional development days equally boring. Candidates who say negative things about their professors and student teaching supervisors will probably be the ones who say negative things about their principals and colleagues. Be positive in the interview! No one wants to hire a negative new teacher!

4. How Much Information Do You Share About Yourself With Students During the First Days of School? Why?

Answer a: (elementary teacher) Students should know a little about us. I show a picture of myself when I was in 3rd grade. They love it! I always show a picture of my cat, too, since this leads into a discussion of their pets. I also share that, while I don't have children, I have a nephew and two nieces, and this lets students know that I do like children.

Answer b: (middle and high school) I tend to talk about my experiences in college as an icebreaker. Most students in the school know about the nearby university and its great sports teams, so I talk about how I played trombone in the band at the football games. I talk about my travels and my love of traveling and how seeing the castles in England made me understand more about the history that I teach. I stress that I loved college and hope that they are already thinking about attending college.

ANSWERS TO QUESTIONS THAT
YOU SHOULDN'T BE ASKED BUT MAY BE

The illegal questions were discussed earlier in this book. You may at some point be asked an illegal question, or one that is not illegal but not in the best form either. How do you answer these questions?

First of all, strive to be diplomatic while guiding the interviewer back to the important topics of an interview—your ability to teach students and manage a classroom. If asked about a spouse or children, frame an answer that works in your favor. For example, "By having been my daughter's first teacher, I am so aware of the value of one-on-one tutoring. I will always strive to implement what I learned by teaching my own daughter." Or, "Since my husband doesn't teach, I get a lot of experience explaining teaching things to him. He is great at proofreading my parent newsletters, and he gave a talk to my student teaching class about how engineers use math in the real world." Some people are experts at dodging questions without answering them and discussing another highlight of their experience or college program instead.

If you have had absolutely no experience with a topic or situation in the question, remember that you can talk about strong examples of teaching from when you were a student. Interviewers want to know that your academic background is strong and sharing highlights of some of your best experiences as a student lets the interviewer know that you are aware of best practices in teaching. Since many new teachers begin teaching as they were taught, it may help to let interviewers know about your positive experiences of being taught.

6

Postinterview Follow-Up and Your Next Career Move

After you leave the interview, what comes next? The very first thing to do is to think about how the interview went, to write down what you learned about the position, and to decide if you want the job if offered. Employers are trying desperately to "make the match" between their position and a new hire, and you should be thinking about "the match" from your point of view, as well. What are *you* looking for in a job, and does this position offer it? Some questions to ask include:

1. Was there "truth in advertising" with this position? Will the job be the one advertised and described by the interviewer?
2. Will you have your own classroom and adequate supplies to teach effectively?
3. Do faculty at this school seem happy, productive, and collegial?
4. If interviewed by the principal, do you feel that he or she will be a supportive administrator?
5. Is the district one that will offer you the types of professional development opportunities you seek?
6. Can you afford to live in this district, based on salary vs. cost of living?
7. What is the class workload and is it "doable"? How large are the classes?
8. Do the instructional values of the district mirror your own?
9. Are there opportunities to sponsor extracurricular activities or to coach, if you want to? Must you coach or sponsor an activity to get the job, and are you willing to do that?

THE THANK-YOU NOTE

It is important to write a thank-you note to the interviewer. The note can be
sent via e-mail if you know that the person reads his or her e-mail. Otherwise,
send a typed or handwritten note. If handwritten, your penmanship should be
good! This note can be succinct:

Ms. Clarice Martin:

I am writing to thank you for the opportunity to interview at your school on
Monday the 6th. After seeing the building and meeting three of the teachers, I
am even more interested in this position than before my interview. I think that
your school is doing remarkable work, especially with the learners' workshop
programs, and I would like to be a part of your faculty.

  I look forward to hearing from you with regard to this position and thank you
again for your time and consideration.

Sincerely,
Karen Smitheley

FOLLOW-UP CALLS

Before you exit the interview, you should be told when hiring decisions will
be finalized. If not, you should ask. When told of the hiring framework, you
should not call before the elapsed time to inquire if a decision has been made.
This tries the patience of support staff (secretaries) and of principals. If you
call two or three times a week asking about a decision, your overpersistence
may result in you being put lower on the list for consideration for the job. Patience is a virtue. If they tell you when they will get back to you, allow that
time frame to pass before calling.

WHAT TO DO IF YOU ARE TRYING
FOR SEVERAL POSITIONS AT ONCE

If your certification is in a high-needs field, or if you live in an area experiencing student growth and teacher shortages, you may be lucky enough to be
a finalist for more than one position. If this is the case, there are some un-
written rules to remember.

  1. Don't count your chickens before they are hatched. In other words,
     don't turn down an offer thinking that a better one is guaranteed by a

principal who gave you some positive comments as you exited an interview. An offer is only an offer when it is given as such.

2. Once you accept an offer, verbally or in writing, that is considered a contract. Neighboring districts have administrators who talk with each other, and saying you will take a job and then not doing so can hurt your professional reputation. Signing a contract and then not following through with it can put you into a legal battle. Be sure before you sign on the dotted line.

3. Can you use an offer from one district to negotiate with another? Some candidates use a job offer from one school as leverage to call another school and push them for an offer. In some districts where employers have more latitude with hiring decisions, this might work. However, in large districts with set procedures, most administrators will say that they cannot change their hiring timeline. In this case, you will have to decide on the offer in your hand versus the offer not yet made. How much are you willing to gamble? Additionally, principals are not in a position to counsel you. You are an adult and have to decide for yourself.

4. If you know that the job is not for you, should you gracefully withdraw? Employers like honesty, and need to know who the real candidates are. It is not only acceptable, but recommended, that you let a potential employer know in writing that you are withdrawing from their search if you know that you would not accept an offer. After the interview, you may write a thank-you letter that informs the employer that you are withdrawing. Always be diplomatic. You do not have to state the reason why, just the fact that you are withdrawing your application. If you recently accepted another offer, you may want to say that, but you do not have to explain your withdrawal.

HOW TO ACCEPT AN OFFER

While employers want you to demonstrate professionalism, they also want to hire enthusiastic, excited new teachers. If you know that this is the job for you, you may accept on the phone when the offer is extended. If you need to consider the offer, ask when your decision needs to be determined. If you do not accept immediately, the employer will probably ask what questions you still have. They may invite you back to the school for another visit. They may be frustrated by your response, and indicate that they need to know within 24 hours. All of these reactions are possible, especially when some schools are struggling to staff all of their openings.

When an offer is made, there is little room for negotiation. Salary, benefits, and workload should have been made clear in the interview. Unlike in the business world, school districts don't really negotiate. Some teachers may attempt to negotiate at this point. For example, if having a classroom was not promised during the interview, a teacher may request that this become part of the package before he or she can accept the offer. The truth is, most employers in education simply cannot make a lot of promises because student numbers and funding are out of their control. Be wary of a potential employer who says something during the job offer conversation that was *not* indicated during the interview.

Once you do accept an offer, there will be more paperwork. At this point, many districts require another official set of college transcripts and confirmation of your teaching certificate. Each district will have its own set of paperwork, which may include a criminal background check, a physical exam or proof of immunizations, and completion of the district's tax and insurance paperwork. Once hired, be sure to read everything sent to you by the district, and to keep your contact information updated if you move. While not a part of your formal evaluation, how you conduct yourself from the moment hired to the first day of school becomes part of your professional reputation. While every teacher has a reputation, you want yours to be positive and professional!

YOUR NEXT JOB SEARCH

It has been said that your first day at a new job is also the first day of your next job search. While that sounds cynical, there is some truth to it. In your first teaching job, you are building your reputation, as well as your repertoire of teaching skills. By taking advantage of professional development opportunities, by serving on committees, and by building a network of colleagues, you are not only becoming better at your current job, but are improving your chances of getting your next job.

What are some specific things to do that will enhance your teaching career and make the next search easier?

1. Keep good records. Take pictures of bulletin boards and of students working in your classroom. Keep these in a portfolio, with dates and related lesson plans.
2. Keep samples of exemplary student work for your next portfolio.
3. Whenever you create original worksheets, quizzes, and exams, keep copies.
4. Document the professional development workshops attended, as well as your volunteer work for the school. Add this to your résumé.

5. Keep your résumé updated, or at least keep a file with the items that need to be added to your résumé when time permits.

6. Work on an advanced degree. Earning a master's degree adds several thousand dollars to your base salary, and may qualify you to be a department chair or to take another leadership position.

7. Don't make enemies—build a network of colleagues who support your work. After you have worked in a teaching position, you will need to update your résumé and list of references, and you will need your current principal, department chair, and colleagues to be those references.

8. Join professional associations, read their journals, and attend their conferences. In other words, stay current in your field.

9. Remember to concentrate on the positive in your next job search. No employer wants to hear that you are leaving your current teaching job because it was too hard, the students were unteachable, the principal was unbearable, or the other teachers weren't good colleagues. Even if these things *are* true, find a better way to explain why you are job searching. For example, "I knew that I would probably only be in the Long Branch community for a year or two, and that for both personal and professional reasons I have always wanted to teach in your district."

Does staying only a year in a first teaching job look bad on a résumé? It may, or it may not, since it all depends on why that job was just for a year. People who job switch often have reputations for not staying—past behavior is the best predictor of future performance. However, some new teachers must take a one-year position in order to find their first job. Every new teacher will have challenges, and the second year is almost always better than the first. Unless you have a specific reason for leaving after one year, try to stay longer for your résumé. Leaving *during* the first year is generally a red flag for employers that you couldn't handle the stress of teaching.

A CHECKLIST FOR GETTING FROM HIRING TO THE FIRST DAY OF SCHOOL

1. Sign your contract and return it in a timely manner. Most contracts state that if you delay, you are at risk of not getting the job.

2. Read and complete all other paperwork from the district human resources office.

3. Organize your personal life. Find a place to live, arrange for childcare, and take care of all the "living arrangement" issues well before new teacher orientation.

4. When invited to new teacher orientation, make it a priority, whether you are paid to attend or not. First impressions are lasting ones, and being late for an orientation meeting makes an administrator wonder if you will be on time to teach.

5. Participate in the orientation meetings. *Do not* take cell phone calls, send e-mails on your BlackBerry, or sit in the back and try to read during these meetings. Learn about the system and become acquainted with your new colleagues at these meetings.

6. Get to know your mentor, if one is assigned to you. Ask this person questions about their role, how often you will meet with them, and if they will be observing your classes. Some mentors are truly guardian angels and can help you thrive the first year, instead of just survive.

7. Find out about the district's mandated curriculum. In other words, what will you be teaching? Which textbooks are available?

8. Find out about grading and testing. What are the school's policies and how are they to be implemented?

9. Know whom to contact if you are sick. This is critically important for the day you wake up with a temperature of 102.

10. Find out where the teaching supplies are kept. Will you have a computer or several in your classroom?

11. As soon as you can, work in your classroom to organize it. Count the desks and compare the number of desks to the number of students on your class roster. No one else will do this for you—and you want every student to have a desk the first day of class!

12. Write your classroom management plan on a big poster for your room and create a letter with the plan to distribute to parents and students.

13. Plan thoroughly for the first day of student attendance. Have seating charts ready and have name cards on the desks of younger students. Spend some time the first day having students get to know each other with interest inventories and get-acquainted activities. Keep students busy the first day, creating a businesslike atmosphere in your room from the start. Teach your management plan and begin to teach classroom routines the first day.

14. Read at least one book on preparing for the first day of school. See the bibliography for a listing of these books.

15. Find and bookmark several good websites to use as references.

16. Before the first day of student attendance, make sure you know the name of at least two teachers who teach nearby, so that you can run to them with last-minute questions.

17. Get a good night's sleep and go to school a little early the first day to check your mailbox (both literally and electronically). Read the messages you receive.

18. Smile and welcome students to your class. You get to be very excited about the first day of school. After all, this is why you worked so hard in college and why you worked so hard in your job search.
19. Enjoy your job and celebrate your successes. They are well-deserved.

WHAT'S NEXT IN YOUR CAREER?

Once you have survived the first couple of years in your classroom, what's next? Are there any career ladders for teachers? What helps teachers to stay in the profession, growing and learning? While some teachers thrive on being a 2nd-grade teacher in the same room and the same school for decades, other teachers need change in order to stay fresh and rejuvenated. While administration is an option (see chapter 1), what's available for teachers who don't want to become school administrators?

Advanced Degree Work

If you start your teaching career with a bachelor's degree and full certification, should you pursue a master's degree, and, if so, in what? Just over half of all teachers nationwide hold a master's degree. A pay raise for earning a master's degree can add several thousand dollars to your annual salary, and when one is paid more for doing the same job, that is worth pursuing, especially since an advanced degree may also help you to be a better teacher.

Master's degrees for teachers are offered in grade level teaching, such as a master's in elementary education, middle grades education, or secondary education. You may also choose to pursue a degree in your subject field (math, science, social studies, special education, Spanish, etc.), administration, or a specialty area, such as reading or English as a second language. Decide what you want to do with this degree before starting it. If your interest is to stay in the classroom teaching French, then improving your command of French is the best area for a master's degree. If you are considering administration, then a master's in that is a must. Some people choose a master's degree in order to stay in teaching, but to do so at a different level or in a different setting, such as becoming a reading specialist, or changing from middle school to elementary teaching.

Finding a program can be a challenge, as you may not live within commuting distance to a college or university. Always ask about summer offerings and online courses when searching for a graduate school. Check the accreditation of the college offering the degree, as some state boards of education will not recognize degrees earned at, and therefore not pay the raise to teachers who earn a degree at, a lesser-known or online college.

You can begin searching for graduate schools by going online and reading the offerings of colleges and universities on their websites. You might want to try www.findtherightschool.com. Talking to colleagues about the programs they completed may yield inside information about the difficulty and practicality of the course work.

National Board Certification

National Board Certification is governed by the National Board for Professional Teaching Standards (NBPTS), a nongovernmental agency established in 1987. NBPTS strives to raise the standards of what accomplished teachers should know and be able to do. The organization offers a rigorous assessment process that leads successful candidates to earn the title of National Board Certified Teacher (NBCT). Any teacher with a bachelor's degree and three years of full-time teaching experience is eligible to apply. In 2006, the assessment fee for participation in the program was $2,500. At least one state, North Carolina, pays the fee for a certain number of candidates every year.

How can adding NBCT after your name be a good thing for you as a teacher? In addition to the higher level of professional recognition, teachers who earn National Board Certification can receive pay raises for doing so in some states. Go to www.nbpts.org and click on your state to see what funding scholarships and incentives are available.

Many educators feel that National Board Certified Teachers have a better understanding of teaching and are highly committed to student learning. These teachers think systematically about the practice of teaching and learn and grow as professionals. The whole idea behind National Board Certification is to raise the level of professionalism for teachers. As of 2006, nearly 50,000 teachers in the United States had earned the distinction of National Board Certification (NBPTS, 2006).

Teachers who work toward National Board Certification begin in their own classrooms. An extensive portfolio, videos, and much documentation of student learning are needed to complete the written assessment successfully. Candidates work on their portfolios for up to one school year. Additionally, candidates must complete a series of exercises in an assessment center to gain certification. The certification is awarded for a period of 10 years, but is renewable by the completion of additional assessments. All application materials are available online at www.nbpts.org.

Teachers with advanced degrees and/or National Board Certification are usually the first ones to be asked to supervise student teachers or to mentor new teachers. Many teachers feel that working with education students and novice teachers is a way to improve and "give back" to the profession. Teachers with experience and advanced degrees become department chairs, lead teachers in grade levels, and committee chairs. When one is able to make decisions and effect change through leadership roles, empowerment follows. Teachers who feel that they are empowered and making positive changes tend not to burn out, and remain in the profession. Sometimes unpaid leadership roles in committees or in the school building lead to new positions with higher pay. While few actual career ladders exist in teaching, a well-educated and dedicated teacher can find paths in the profession that are very rewarding. It can be said that the best teaching path may be that stated by Christa McAuliffe, the first teacher in space: "I touch the future; I teach."

Appendix A

Sample Interview Questions by Grade and Subject Area

PRESCHOOL QUESTIONS

1. Explain a task that might be developmentally inappropriate for a 3-year-old, yet could be done easily by an older student.
2. What have you done in the past to help a child who is frustrated that he or she cannot complete a task that others in the class can accomplish?
3. What are tried-and-true ways to get the attention of young children?
4. What special safety precautions must be considered when working with the youngest students (2-, 3-, 4-year-olds)?
5. What kinds of rules and consequences have you implemented in a classroom for 4-year-olds?
6. What do young children consider to be rewards?
7. Tell me about a time when a child tested the limits you set. What did you do and what were the results?

FOR KINDERGARTEN, GRADES 1, 2

1. Describe ways to get students interested in reading.
2. How have you taught reading in the past?
3. Have you experienced teaching with both phonics and whole language? If so, please describe.
4. Name and describe any specific reading package that you have taught with in the past (for example, directed reading instruction or a specific textbook publisher).
5. Describe how you have used manipulatives to teach a math lesson.

6. Some researchers say that boys develop very differently in these grades than girls. How have you adapted lessons to meet boys' needs?

7. How have you incorporated play into these grades?

GRADES 3–5

1. Tell about how you have prepared students for standardized tests.

2. Describe your experiences with anecdotal records or running records to assess student achievement.

3. Describe how your classroom can be a print-rich environment for students.

4. How do you transition students from one activity/subject to the next successfully?

5. Students this age need to move. How have you incorporated movement into your classes?

6. Describe a specific social studies unit that you have implemented.

7. Describe a specific science unit that you have taught.

8. How have you integrated subjects together in lessons?

9. Describe writing activities that have worked well for this age group.

MIDDLE SCHOOL–SPECIFIC QUESTIONS—GRADES 6–8

1. Tell me about a time when you have worked on a teaching team.

2. Describe your experiences of working in a "school within a school" concept.

3. Share an example you have seen or used for integrating writing across the curriculum.

4. How have you integrated math into other subject areas?

5. The improvement of students' reading skills is important during middle school. Tell about your experiences teaching reading directly, or how you have integrated reading strategies into other subject areas.

6. Games can be intrinsically motivating to middle grades students. How have you used games to motivate students in your classes? Have you encountered problems with the use of games, and how did you resolve the problems?

7. What is a typical concern/worry that middle school students bring to their teachers as advisors/counselors, and how have you dealt with such a concern?

8. Adolescents need time for talking and expressing their opinions. How have you built time into your day to allow students to discuss opinions, talk about topics of interest, and to "vent" their frustrations?

9. Do you have a special skill or interest that you have shared with students in an exploratory class or homeroom?

HIGH SCHOOL–SPECIFIC QUESTIONS

1. How have you interested students in your subject field?
2. Give an example of how you can relate your subject to something of relevance to today's teenagers.
3. How have you supplemented the textbook in your classes?
4. What is a current trend in the teaching of this subject and how have you dealt with this trend?
5. How have you encouraged students to stay in high school and graduate?
6. What kinds of stressors do today's high school students face, and how have you helped them cope with their concerns?
7. Describe the teaching experiences you have had with traditional 50-minute classes and with blocked scheduling.
8. How have you successfully prepared students for standardized tests, graduation tests, or end-of-course tests?
9. How have you supported students or become better acquainted with students through extracurricular activities?
10. How have you integrated technology into your high school classes? What has worked well with students?

English

1. How have you kept students interested in reading in your classes?
2. Describe a project or group work that has been successful with your students.
3. How have you been able to get students' work read by outside audiences?
4. How have you incorporated study skills for the ACT/SAT tests into your classes?
5. How have you dealt with the variance in reading skills in your classroom?
6. Describe your experiences teaching vocabulary and grammar.

Mathematics

1. How have you gained and kept students' interest in mathematics?
2. How have you implemented and used calculators and other technology in your classes?

3. How have you assessed a new class with regard to their previous math skills?
4. How do you handle homework issues in the math class? Are students allowed to work together? Can they get outside help? Explain your homework policy to me as if you were explaining it to your classes.

Science

1. Tell about the use of labs in science classes that you have taught.
2. Tell about your teaching experience in biology with regard to the evolution/creationism debate.
3. How have you motivated students to take advanced science classes?

Social Studies/History

1. What teaching strategies/methods have you employed to teach lessons, other than lectures?
2. How have you created interest in the study of history?
3. How have you accommodated or helped weak readers with the social studies/history readings required in your classes?

Foreign Languages/World Languages

1. What percentage of a typical lesson is taught in the target language? Why?
2. Describe your experiences teaching grammar.
3. Describe a sample cultural lesson or unit you have used with a class.
4. Describe your experiences with students who are native speakers in your classes. How are native speakers a challenge and a help in the class?
5. How have you enabled students to use the target language outside of class or for a larger audience?

Art

1. How have you helped students who aren't necessarily artistically gifted?
2. How have you shown students' work to a larger audience than the class?
3. Describe how you have worked with regular classroom teachers to ensure that the time for art isn't diminished.
4. How have you established grading scales for your art classes?
5. What special considerations for safety and clean-up are part of the art room, and how have you successfully implemented procedures for your room?

Health and Physical Education

1. How have you built obesity and weight consciousness topics into your courses?
2. How have you encouraged students who are not in shape to succeed in activities?
3. Describe your experiences managing large groups of students, or with managing students in a large space (gym or field).
4. Describe your coaching experiences.
5. Describe a time when a student was dropped or cut from a team sport and a parent complained to you about this.

SPECIAL EDUCATION QUESTIONS (ALL GRADE LEVELS)

Populations

1. Describe your past experiences with exceptional learners. Be specific.
2. Describe your experiences with students exhibiting ADD and ADHD. What strategies were most effective for those students?
3. Describe your work with students exhibiting marked impulsivity.
4. Describe your work with students experiencing _____ (insert a specific disability here).

Settings

1. Describe your experiences with mainstreaming as a special education teacher working with a classroom teacher.
2. Describe your experiences with full inclusion as a special education teacher working with a classroom teacher.
3. Describe your experiences as a teacher in a pull-out program.
4. Describe how you have worked with other professionals to help a student through collaborative consultation.
5. Describe your work with one student's IEP (Individualized Education Program).

Methods

1. Describe how you have incorporated technology into lessons for exceptional children.
2. How have you modified lessons for exceptional learners?
3. How have you modified tests for exceptional learners?

4. How have you modified a physical environment feature to assist a child?

Communication

1. Describe a parent conference that you have observed or participated in regarding an exceptional child. What went well? What would you change?
2. Describe a positive meeting between a special education teacher and a classroom teacher about a specific child. What went well? What would you change?

QUESTIONS FOR PROVISIONALLY OR NON–FULLY CERTIFIED TEACHERS (ANY GRADE LEVEL)

Candidates who are not fully certified may be asked the regular set of questions for their grade level. However, if you are entering teaching through a test-out option, a program where you did not student teach, or a program where you begin teaching and then take course work, you simply will not know the answers to BBI-type questions.

When asked these questions, you may consider referring back to your own school experiences. For example, if asked about how to manage a classroom, you could describe how one of your teachers was an excellent manager, stating that you would strive to build a community of learners as he or she had. When asked about how you might teach your subject matter, you can describe activities from classes that you remember that were effectively taught.

The following questions are designed for prospective teachers who are entering the job market through nontraditional/alternative paths to education and may have had little or no experience with teaching.

Entrance Into Teaching

1. Why are you choosing to enter teaching through a provisional route, without being fully certified?
2. What personal characteristics and background do you possess that will help you to succeed in teaching?

Education, Past and Present

1. Tell me about your bachelor's degree and the specifics of your knowledge of the subject(s) you will teach.

2. Describe your route to provisional certification—testing, course work, and field experiences. Now describe your proposed route to full certification.
3. What experiences in classrooms have you had with students this age?
4. What experiences have you had with students of this age outside of classrooms?
5. What are you currently reading and studying to learn about the trends and issues in education and in your subject-matter field(s)?

Past Work Experience

1. In your previous jobs, what types of organizational skills did you use?
2. Tell about a time when you planned and implemented an activity, meeting, or event.
3. What kinds of assessment did you conduct in your previous work?
4. How did you know that you were successful in your past job?
5. Tell about communications you implemented with your past boss and peers.
6. Tell about experiences that you have had establishing and enforcing rules in a work setting.
7. Describe your role in being a leader or innovator in your previous jobs.

About the Teaching Profession

1. What does the general public believe about education, teachers, and schools? What do you believe about education, teachers, and schools?
2. If you were to encounter negativity on the part of other teachers in your building because you are not fully certified, how might you combat that negativity?
3. What is your response to this statement: "Teaching is an easy job for those who want to work from 8 to 4, Monday through Friday."

QUESTIONS BASED ON THE INTASC STANDARDS

Many colleges of education build their teacher education programs on the standards set forth by the Interstate New Teacher Assessment and Support Consortium (INTASC). (See, for example, Parkay and Stanford, in the reference list.) Some savvy administrators might want to take the 10 standards and ask questions based on those. You will see that many of these questions were covered by the general questions in chapter 5 of this book. The bottom line is that answers to questions that are based on the standards will showcase your knowledge, skills, disposition, and experience in teaching. If you can successfully answer these questions, it is indeed an indicator of your future performance.

Knowledge of Subject Matter

The teacher understands the central concepts, tools of inquiry, and structures of the subject being taught and can create learning experiences that make these aspects of subject matter meaningful for students.

1. Describe an activity, lesson, or project that your students have done that was successful and explain why it was successful.
2. Describe a topic considered hard to teach in your field and a lesson that you have used that students enjoyed on this topic.

Knowledge of Human Development and Learning

The teacher understands how children learn and develop, and can provide learning opportunities that support their intellectual, social, and personal development.

1. Describe an activity or lesson that was successful with an age group that you have taught, then explain why this same lesson would not work with older or younger students.
2. Describe a lesson where you have integrated a social skill into an academic lesson.

Adapting Instruction for Individual Needs

The teacher understands how students differ in their approaches to learning and creates instructional opportunities that are adapted to diverse learners.

1. Describe a lesson that you have taught that combined auditory, visual, and/or kinesthetic teaching strategies.
2. Describe modifications that you have made to an assignment or test so that a student could master the material successfully in spite of an exceptionality.

Multiple Instructional Strategies

The teacher uses various instructional strategies to encourage students' development of critical thinking, problem-solving, and performance skills.

1. Describe a lesson where you used higher-order questions to challenge students.
2. Describe an activity that you have implemented where students "do" something with material from a textbook other than just answer questions.

Classroom Motivation and Management

The teacher uses an understanding of individual and group motivation and behavior to create a learning environment that encourages positive social interaction, active engagement in learning, and self-motivation.

1. How do you set up a classroom routine to facilitate "time on task"?
2. Describe how your classroom management plan has worked to improve the behavior of an individual student.

Communication Skills

The teacher uses knowledge of effective verbal, nonverbal, and media communication techniques to foster active inquiry, collaboration, and supportive interaction in the classroom.

1. Explain how you have used technology or other visuals to enhance a lesson.
2. How can you tell that students hear and understand your directions, lesson input, and questions?

Instructional Planning Skills

The teacher plans instruction based upon knowledge of subject matter, the students, the community, and curriculum goals.

1. Describe a state or national standard in your subject field and how you planned a lesson to meet that standard.
2. Tell about your long-term planning. How do you plan a unit, keeping national, state, and district goals in mind?

Assessment of Student Learning

The teacher understands and uses formal and informal assessment strategies to evaluate and ensure the continuous intellectual, social, and physical development of the learner.

1. Describe a grading scale that works well for one subject in your grade area.
2. Besides written tests, how have you assessed student work?

Professional Commitment and Responsibility

The teacher is a reflective practitioner who continually evaluates the effects of his or her choices and actions on others (students, parents, and other professionals in the learning community) and who actively seeks out opportunities to grow professionally.

1. In college or during your previous teaching experiences, what course or professional development opportunity has been most beneficial to you? Why?
2. In what organizations do you maintain membership and what materials do you read to stay current in your field?

Partnerships

1. Describe positive parent involvement or community involvement programs that you have worked with or observed.
2. Describe a successful way to communicate with colleagues or with a principal.

Appendix B

GETTING YOUR STATE TEACHING LICENSE

- www.abcte.org
- www.professionalteacher.com
- www.uky.edu/Education/TEP/usacert.html

NO CHILD LEFT BEHIND

- www.ed.gov/nclb/landing.jhtml
- www.teacherquality.us

JOB SEARCHING

- www.abcteachingjobs.com
- www.educationamerica.net
- www.k12jobs.com
- www.nationjob.com/education
- www.teacherjobs.com
- www.teachers-teachers.com
- www.teaching-jobs.org

TEACHING ABROAD

- www.cie.uci.edu/iop/teaching.html
- www.eslcafe.com/jobs
- www.joyjobs.com
- overseasdigest.com/teacher8.html
- www.teachabroad.com
- www.tefl.com

PROFESSIONAL ORGANIZATIONS BY DISCIPLINE

- Art education: www.naea-reston.org
- English: www.ncte.org
- Foreign languages: www.actfl.org
- History: www.sscnet.ucla.edu/nchs
- International Reading Association: www.reading.org
- Math: www.nctm.org
- Middle school: www.nmsa.org
- Music education: www.menc.org
- Physical education: www.aahperd.org/naspe
- Science: www.nsta.org
- Social studies: www.ncss.org
- Special education: www.naset.org

PROFESSIONAL ASSOCIATIONS FOR ALL TEACHERS

- American Federation of Teachers, www.aft.org
- Kappa Delta Pi, www.kdp.org
- National Board for Professional Teaching Standards, www.nbpts.org
- National Education Association, www.nea.org
- Phi Delta Kappa, www.pdkintl.org

CLASSROOM MANAGEMENT

- www.disciplineassociates.com
- www.disciplinehelp.com
- www.effectiveteaching.com
- www.fredjones.com
- www.teachersworkshop.com

LESSON IDEAS/PLANNING/CURRICULUM

- abcteach.com
- www.academicbenchmarks.com (for state standards)
- www.brains.org
- www.curriculumdesigners.com (for Heidi Hayes Jacobs' work)
- www.lessonplanspage.com
- www.schoolexpress.com
- www.teacherplanet.com
- www.teaching-point.net
- www.teachnet.com

BOOKS FOR NEW TEACHERS

- www.corwinpress.com
- www.kdp.org
- www.rowmaneducation.com

Bibliography

CLASSROOM MANAGEMENT AND DISCIPLINE

Brady, K., Forton, M. B., Porter, D., & Wood, C. (2003). *Rules in school*. Greenfield, MA: Northeast Foundation for Children.

Burden, P. (2006). *Classroom management: Creating a successful K–12 learning community* (3rd ed.). Hoboken, NJ: Wiley.

Canter, L. (2006). *Classroom management for academic success*. Bloomington, IN: Solution Tree.

Canter, L. & Canter, M. (2001). *Assertive discipline: Positive behavior management for today's classroom* (3rd ed.). Los Angeles: Canter and Associates.

Clement, M. C. (2005). *First time in the high school classroom: Essential guide for the new teacher*. Lanham, MD: Rowman & Littlefield Education.

Clark, R. (2003). *The essential 55: An award-winning educator's rules for discovering the successful student in every child*. New York: Hyperion.

Clark, R. (2004). *The excellent 11: Qualities teachers and parents use to motivate, inspire, and educate children*. New York: Hyperion.

Emmer, E. T., Evertson, C. M., & Worsham, M. E. (2006). *Classroom management for middle and high school teachers* (7th ed.). Boston: Pearson, Allyn & Bacon.

Evertson, C. M., Emmer, E. T., & Worsham, M. E. (2006). *Classroom management for elementary teachers* (7th ed.). Boston: Pearson, Allyn & Bacon.

Jones, F. H. (2000). *Tools for teaching: Discipline, instruction, motivation*. Santa Cruz, CA: Fredric H. Jones & Associates.

Jones, V. F., & Jones, L. (2007). *Comprehensive classroom management: Creating communities of support and solving problems*. Boston: Pearson, Allyn & Bacon.

Marshall, M. (2001). *Discipline without stress, punishments, or rewards: How teachers and parents promote responsibility and learning*. Los Alamitos, CA: Piper Press.

Mendler, A. N. (2005*). Just in time: Powerful strategies to promote positive behavior*. Bloomington, IN: National Educational Service.

Wong, H. K. & Wong, R. T. (2005). *The first days of school: How to be an effective teacher* (3rd ed.). Mountain View, CA: Harry K. Wong.

CURRICULUM AND METHODS

Jacobs, H. H. (1997). *Mapping the big picture: Integrating curriculum and assessment, K–12*. Alexandria, VA: Association for Supervision and Curriculum Development.

Jacobs, H. H. (2004). *Getting results with curriculum mapping*. Alexandria, VA: Association for Supervision and Curriculum Development.

Marzano, R. J., Norford, J. S., Paynter, D. E., Pickering, D. J., & Gaddy, B. B. (2005). *A handbook for classroom instruction that works*. Upper Saddle River, NJ: Pearson/Prentice Hall.

Marzano, R. J., Pickering, D. J., & Pollock, J. E. (2005). *Classroom instruction that works*. Upper Saddle River, NJ: Pearson/Prentice Hall.

Tomlinson, C. A. & McTighe, J. (2006). *Integrating differentiated instruction and understanding by design: Connecting content and kids*. Alexandria, VA: Association for Supervision and Curriculum Development.

JUST FOR ELEMENTARY TEACHERS

Denton, P. & Kriete, R. (2000). *The first six weeks of school*. Greenfield, MA: Northeast Foundation for Children.

FOR TEACHERS OF MIDDLE GRADES

Wormeli, R. (2001). *Meet me in the middle: Becoming an accomplished middle-level teacher*. Portland, ME: Stenhouse.

Wormeli, R. (2003). *Day one and beyond: Practical matters for new middle-level teachers*. Portland, ME: Stenhouse.

FOR HIGH SCHOOL TEACHERS

Clement, M. C. (2003). *But high school teaching is different!: Success strategies for new secondary teachers*. Washington, DC: National Education Association.

FOR ALL NEW TEACHERS

Clement, M. C. (1997). *Bright ideas: A pocket mentor for beginning teachers*. Washington, DC: National Education Association.

Enz, B. J., Kortman, S. A., & Honaker, C. J. (2003). *Ready, set, teach!: A winning design for your first year*. Indianapolis, IN: Kappa Delta Pi.

Fuery, C. (2005). *The new winning year one: Jump-start student success from day one, K–12: An essential survival guide for new and veteran teachers*. Captiva, FL: Sanibel SandDollar.

Glanz, J. (2004). *Teaching 101: Classroom strategies for the beginning teacher*. Thousand Oaks, CA: Corwin.

Kronowitz, E. L. (2004). *Your first year of teaching and beyond*. Boston: Pearson, Allyn & Bacon.

Rethinking Schools. (2004). *The new teacher book*. Milwaukee, WI: Rethinking Schools Ltd.

PORTFOLIOS

Campbell, D. M., Cignetti, P. B., Melenyzer, B. J., Nettles, D. H., & Wyman, R. M. (2004). *How to develop a professional portfolio: A manual for teachers*. Boston: Pearson, Allyn & Bacon.

Kilbane, C. R. & Milman, N. B. (2003). *The digital teaching portfolio handbook: A how-to guide for educators*. Boston: Allyn & Bacon.

SUBSTITUTE TEACHING

Fuery, C. (1998). *Successful subbing: A survival guide to help you teach like a pro*. Sanibel Island, FL: Sanibel SandDollar.

References

American Association for Employment in Education. (2006). *Job search handbook for educators*. Columbus, OH: AAEE.

Breaux, A. L. & Wong, H. K. (2003). *New teacher induction: How to train, support, and retain new teachers*. Mountain View, CA: Harry K. Wong.

Ingersoll, R. M. (2003). The teacher shortage: Myth or reality? *Educational Horizons* 81(3): 146–152.

National Board for Professional Teaching Standards. (2006). *2006 Guide to National Board Certification*. Available online at www.nbpts.org.

Parkay, F. W. & Stanford, B. H. (2003). *Becoming a teacher* (6th ed.). Boston: Allyn & Bacon.

Ryan, R. (2000). *60 seconds and you're hired!* New York: Penguin.

U. S. Department of Education. (2004). *No child left behind: A toolkit for teachers*. Washington, DC: USDOE.

About the Author

Mary C. Clement was a high school foreign language teacher for eight years before earning a doctorate in curriculum and instruction from the University of Illinois at Urbana-Champaign. For six years she directed the Beginning Teacher Program at Eastern Illinois University, teaching seminars for new teachers and leading workshops for administrators about hiring and inducting new teachers. Since 1997 she has been a professor of teacher education at Berry College, northwest of Atlanta, Georgia.

Clement is the author of *Building the Best Faculty, So You Want to Be a Teacher?, First Time in the High School Classroom*, and *The ABC's of Job-Hunting for Teachers*. Her articles have appeared in the *Phi Delta Kappan, Principal Leadership, The American School Board Journal*, and Kappa Delta Pi's *Educational Forum* and *Record*. Her campus seminars and conference presentations have helped hundreds of aspiring new teachers find jobs.